D1592528

INTERVENTIONS

Conor Cunningham and Peter Candler

GENERAL EDITORS

It's not a question of whether one believes in God or not. Rather, it's a question of if, in the absence of God, we can have belief, any belief.

"If you live today," wrote Flannery O'Connor, "you breathe in nihilism." Whether "religious" or "secular," it is "the very gas you breathe." Both within and without the academy, there is an air common to both deconstruction and scientism — both might be described as species of *reductionism*. The dominance of these modes of knowledge in popular and professional discourse is quite incontestable, perhaps no more so where questions of theological import are often subjugated to the margins of intellectual respectability. Yet it is precisely the proponents and defenders of religious belief in an age of nihilism that are often among those most — unwittingly or not — complicit in this very reduction. In these latter cases, one frequently spies an accommodationist impulse, whereby our concepts must be first submitted to a prior philosophical court of appeal in order for them to render any intellectual value. To cite one particularly salient example, debates over the origins, nature, and ends of human life are routinely partitioned off into categories of "evolutionism" and "creationism," often with little nuance. Where attempts to mediate these arguments are to be found, frequently the strategy is that of a kind of accommodation: How can we adapt our belief in creation to an already established evolutionary metaphysic, or, how can we have our evolutionary cake and eat it too? It is sadly the case that, despite the best intentions of such "intellectual ecumenism," the distinctive voice of theology is the first one to succumb to aphony — either from impetuous overuse or from a deliberate silencing.

The books in this unique new series propose no such simple accommodation. They rather seek and perform tactical interventions in such debates in a manner that problematizes the accepted terms of such debates. They propose something altogether more demanding: through a kind of refusal of the disciplinary isolation now standard in modern universities, a genuinely interdisciplinary series of mediations of crucial concepts and key figures in contemporary thought. These volumes will attempt to discuss these topics as they are articulated within their own field, including their historical emergence, and cultural significance, which will provide a way into seemingly abstract discussions. At the same time, they aim to analyze what consequences such thinking may have for theology, both positive and negative, and, in light of these new perspectives, to develop an effective response — one that will better situate students of theology and professional theologians alike within the most vital debates informing Western society, and so increase their understanding of, participation in, and contribution to these.

To a generation brought up on a diet of deconstruction, on the one hand, and scientism, on the other, Interventions offers an alternative that is *otherwise than nihilistic* — doing so by approaching well-worn questions and topics, as well as historical and contemporary figures, from an original and interdisciplinary angle, and so avoid having to steer a course between the aforementioned Scylla and Charybdis.

This series will also seek to navigate not just through these twin dangers, but also through the dangerous "and" that joins them. That is to say, it will attempt to be genuinely interdisciplinary in avoiding the conjunctive approach to such topics that takes as paradigmatic a relationship of "theology and phenomenology" or "religion and science." Instead, the volumes in this series will, in general, attempt to treat such discourses not as discrete disciplines unto themselves, but as moments within a distended theological performance. Above all, they will hopefully contribute to a renewed atmosphere shared by theologians and philosophers (not to mention those in other disciplines) — an air that is not nothing.

CENTRE OF THEOLOGY AND PHILOSOPHY

(www.theologyphilosophycentre.co.uk)

Every doctrine which does not reach the one thing necessary, every separated philosophy, will remain deceived by false appearances. It will be a doctrine, it will not be Philosophy.

Maurice Blondel, 1861-1949

This book series is the product of the work carried out at the Centre of Theology and Philosophy (COTP), at the University of Nottingham.

The COTP is a research-led institution organized at the interstices of theology and philosophy. It is founded on the conviction that these two disciplines cannot be adequately understood or further developed, save with reference to each other. This is true in historical terms, since we cannot comprehend our Western cultural legacy unless we acknowledge the interaction of the Hebraic and Hellenic traditions. It is also true conceptually, since reasoning is not fully separable from faith and hope, or conceptual reflection from revelatory disclosure. The reverse also holds, in either case.

The Centre is concerned with:

- the historical interaction between theology and philosophy.
- the current relation between the two disciplines.
- attempts to overcome the analytic/continental divide in philosophy.
- the question of the status of "metaphysics": Is the term used equivocally? Is it now at an end? Or have twentieth-century attempts to have a postmetaphysical philosophy themselves come to an end?
- the construction of a rich Catholic humanism.

I am very glad to be associated with the endeavours of this extremely important Centre that helps to further work of enormous importance. Among its concerns is the question whether modernity is more an interim than a completion — an interim between a pre-modernity in which the porosity between theology and philosophy was granted, perhaps taken for granted, and a postmodernity where their porosity must be unclogged and enacted anew. Through the work of leading theologians of international stature and philosophers whose writings bear on this porosity, the Centre offers an exciting forum to advance in diverse ways this challenging and entirely needful, and cutting-edge work.

Professor William Desmond, Leuven

ŽIŽEK

A (Very) Critical Introduction

Marcus Pound

WILLIAM B. EERDMANS PUBLISHING COMPANY

GRAND RAPIDS, MICHIGAN / CAMBRIDGE, U.K.

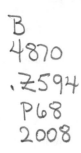
Published 2008 by

Wm. B. Eerdmans Publishing Co.

2140 Oak Industrial Drive N.E., Grand Rapids, Michigan 49505 /

P.O. Box 163, Cambridge CB3 9PU U.K.

Printed in the United States of America

13 12 11 10 09 08   7 6 5 4 3 2 1

Library of Congress Cataloging-in-Publication Data

Pound, Marcus.

Žižek: a (very) critical introduction / Marcus Pound.

p.   cm. — (Interventions)

Includes bibliographical references and index.

ISBN 978-0-8028-6001-9 (pbk. : alk. paper)

1. Žižek, Slavoj.   I. Title.

B4870.Z594P68   2008

199'.4973 — dc22

2008016066

www.eerdmans.com

Theo-logie:

Ελωι ελωι λεμα σαβαχθανι

(Mark 15:34)

Dio-logie:

In questa mancanza,
Bisogna affondare

Pseudo-Hadewijch,
Poesie Miste

Contents

Abbreviations

Works by Žižek

AF   *The Abyss of Freedom/Ages of the World by F. W. J. Schelling.* Ann Arbor: University of Michigan Press, 1997.

C   *Conversations with Žižek.* Cambridge: Polity, 2004.

CHU   with J. Butler and E. Laclau. *Contingency, Hegemony, Universality: Contemporary Dialogues on the Left.* London and New York: Verso, 2000.

DSST   *Did Somebody Say Totalitarianism? Five Interventions in the (Mis) Use of a Notion.* London and New York: Verso, 2001.

EYS   *Enjoy Your Symptom: Jacques Lacan in Hollywood and Out.* 2nd ed. London and New York: Routledge, 2001.

FA   *The Fragile Absolute; or, Why Is the Christian Legacy Worth Fighting For?* London and New York: Verso, 2000.

FTKN   *For They Know Not What They Do: Enjoyment as a Political Factor.* London and New York: Verso, 2002.

IR   *Interrogating the Real.* Edited by Rex Butler and Scott Stephens. London and New York: Continuum, 2005.

L   *How to Read Lacan.* London: Granta Books, 2006.

LA   *Looking Awry: An Introduction to Jacques Lacan through Popular Culture.* Cambridge and London: MIT Press, 1991.

ME   *The Metastasis of Enjoyment: Six Essays on Woman and Causality.* London: Verso, 1994.

OB   *On Belief.* London: Routledge, 2001.

OSD	with M. Dolar. *Opera's Second Death.* London: Routledge, 2002.
PD	*The Puppet and the Dwarf: The Perverse Core of Christianity.* London: MIT Press, 2003.
PF	*The Plague of Fantasies.* London and New York: Verso, 1997.
PV	*The Parallax View.* London: MIT Press, 2006.
RG	*Revolution at the Gates: Selected Writings of Lenin from 1917.* London and New York: Verso, 2002.
SOI	*The Sublime Object of Ideology.* London and New York: Verso, 2002.
TN	*Tarrying with the Negative: Kant, Hegel, and the Critique of Ideology.* Durham, N.C.: Duke University Press, 1993.
TS	*The Ticklish Subject: The Absent Centre of Political Ontology.* London and New York: Verso, 2000.
UE	*The Universal Exception.* Edited by Rex Butler and Scott Stephens. London and New York: Continuum, 2006.
ZR	*The Žižek Reader.* Oxford: Blackwell, 1999.

Works by Freud

| SE | All references are to the *Standard Edition of the Complete Psychological Works of Freud.* Edited and translated by James Strachey, in collaboration with Anna Freud, assisted by Alix Strachey and Alan Tyson. 24 vols. London: Hogarth Press, 1953-1974. |

Works by Lacan

AÉ	*Autres Écrits.* Paris: Seuil, 2001.
É	*Écrits.* Translated by Bruce Fink. New York and London: Norton, 2006. In a typical abbreviation (E, 94/311), the second page reference is to the French edition: Jacques Lacan, *Écrits* (Paris: Seuil, 1966).
NoF	"Introduction to the Names-of-the-Father Seminar." In *Television: A Challenge to the Psychoanalytic Establishment,* edited

by Joan Copjec and translated by Jeffrey Mehlman. New York and London: Norton, 1990.

SI   *The Seminar of Jacques Lacan, I: Freud's Papers on Technique, 1953-1954.* Edited by Jacques-Alain Miller. Translated by John Forrester. London and New York: Norton, 1991.

SII   *The Seminar of Jacques Lacan, II: The Ego in Freud's Theory and in the Technique of Psychoanalysis, 1954-1955.* Edited by Jacques-Alain Miller. Translated by Sylvana Tomaselli. London and New York: Norton, 1991.

SIII *The Seminar of Jacques Lacan, III: Psychosis, 1955-1956.* Edited by Jacques-Alain Miller. Translated by Russell Grigg. London: Routledge, 2000.

SV   *The Seminar of Jacques Lacan, V: The Formations of the Unconscious, 1957-1958.* Translated by Cormac Gallagher. Unpublished.

SVII *The Seminar of Jacques Lacan, VII: The Ethics of Psychoanalysis, 1959-1960.* Edited by Jacques-Alain Miller. Translated by Dennis Porter. London: Routledge, 1999.

SVIII *Le Séminaire Livre VIII: Le Transfert, 1960-1961.* Edited by Jacques-Alain Miller. Paris: Seuil, 1991.

SXI   *The Seminar of Jacques Lacan, XI: The Four Fundamental Concepts of Psycho-analysis, 1963-1964.* Edited by Jacques-Alain Miller. Translated by Alan Sheridan. London: Vintage, 1998.

SXIV *The Seminar of Jacques Lacan: The Logic of Phantasy, 1966-1967.* Translated by Cormac Gallagher. Unpublished.

SXV   *The Seminar of Jacques Lacan, XV: The Psychoanalytic Act, 1967-1968.* Translated by C. Gallagher. Unpublished.

SXVI *The Seminar of Jacques Lacan, XVI: From the Other to the Other, 1968-1969.* Translated by C. Gallagher. Unpublished.

SXX   *The Seminar of Jacques Lacan, XX: On Feminine Sexuality; The Limits of Love and Knowledge, 1972-1973.* Edited by Jacques Alain-Miller. Translated by Bruce Fink. London and New York: Norton, 1998.

T   *Television: A Challenge to the Psychoanalytic Establishment.* Edited by Joan Copjec. Translated by Jeffrey Mehlman. New York and London: Norton, 1990.

Preface

When it comes to relations between church and state, today's Christians find themselves in a strange reversal from the situation of their Roman counterparts.[1] In the first century the problem arose because religious worship could always be directed toward the empire. This is clearly what Josephus recalls regarding Emperor Caligula. Caligula declared himself a god and ordered his statues placed in temples across Europe, a move that sparked the First Jewish Revolt. By contrast, the problem confronting Christians today is that they do not have the power to contest effectively the emperors when they extend the empire in the name of their God, a problem shared by Christians, Jews, and Muslims alike. The same may be said of the current theological turn within Marxism. In the old days Christians had to contend with the Marxist critique of religion, a confrontation that arguably led to one of the most radical theological revolts of recent times: liberation theology, a movement that continues to resonate. Today, however, atheist Marxists such as Slavoj Žižek appear only too happy to extend their project in the name of Christianity, thereby short-circuiting the possibility for a critical theological voice.

What results may be broadly called a "political theology," somewhere in the tradition of Carl Schmitt; a political vision built upon secularized theological concepts.[2] This is not a *believing* politics; Žižek does not ad-

1. Ward Blanton first makes this point in "Disturbing Politics: Neo-Paulinism and the Scrambling of Religious and Secular Identities," *Dialog* 46, no. 1 (2007): 3-13, 6.
2. See, for example, Carl Schmitt, *Political Sovereignty: Four Chapters on the Concept of Sovereignty,* trans. G. Schwab (London: MIT Press, 1985).

vocate a theocracy; nor is he concerned to align religion with any one particular political party such as the Christian Socialists. But neither does it disinherit its theological past.

The trouble with this "political theology" is that it clings to the underlying assumption that there exists a realm of pure nature, i.e., a realm that is void of any supernatural; so any subsequent appeal to Christianity is done so only by refusing already the fundamental Christian claim that man is ordered toward the supernatural, that man has a natural desire for the supernatural. Leaving the supernatural behind does not do away with the need for theology; on the contrary, as Žižek's work highlights, it leads inevitably to a theology, only one of utter abandonment, *a bastard theology without a Father.* The problem arises, then, when one transposes this theology into politics, because when a theology of abandonment becomes a politics of abandonment, it encourages a culture of victimhood (the one abandoned), thereby undermining the possibility for engaged political action.

This introduction aims to critically recover some of the theology underpinning Žižek's work, and in doing so, to make good on Žižek's project: through a return to the theological sources *(ressourcement)* of politics, one is able to repeat a political act.

Acknowledgments

I wish to acknowledge my gratitude and indebtedness to Richard Johnson, who first highlighted to me the theological significance and sheer fun of Žižek's work. Johnson's enthusiasm for the issues, his penetrating mind, and his clarity of exposition have been decisive in formulating and writing this book, along with his direct comments on the text through its various stages. I also thank Conor Cunningham. I am indebted not only to his thought and comments, but also to his generosity of vision which has provided a platform for this work amongst others. Eliana has provided critical discussion concerning many of the points; I owe an intellectual debt of gratitude to her. Robert Pound provided magic along the way. This book was also made possible through the critical and practical commitment to such an engagement spearheaded through the Nottingham Centre of Theology and Philosophy. In this regard I especially thank John Milbank, Conor Cunningham, Pete Candler, the publisher Eerdmans, and those associated with the Centre. This book was written with money made available by Evelyn and Sydney Godfrey Phillips. Lacan would have approved the name of Mr. Phillips's preferred blend of tobacco: *Grand Cut.* This book is dedicated to them. Finally, thanks go to Žižek, whose work has been a constant source of challenge, enjoyment, and suffering.

Introduction

During the London peace march of 2003, held in protest of the war in Iraq, Tony Blair invited the country to rebel, only to quickly add the rejoinder that rebellion *must* be responsible; it amounts to saying, "you can have a revolution, only as long as nothing changes."[1] This very attitude characterizes perfectly the climate of critical reaction to the philosopher Slavoj Žižek: his critics are critical in a responsible manner, offering up a quibble or dispute over particular emphases, while lacking the character of an event; i.e., failing to challenge his system as a whole. The question remains: How does one make such a critical gesture? The wager of this introduction is that one can make such a gesture only from the standpoint of theology. By this I do not simply intend to pit theology against critical theory, as if this were a debate between two opposing camps, because much of Žižek's work is already Christian in diverse and profound ways. Rather, the critical gesture consists in assuming beforehand the animating role of theology in his work; i.e., to read it *as* theology pure and simple, risking the political *for* the theological. To adopt his own tone, one should not take a defensive stance against his work but fully endorse what he claims: that Christianity really *is* worth saving (FA, 2). In this way — by reading him as theology — I argue paradoxically that one recovers what is most politically salient in his work, and in such a way as to answer many of the criticisms leveled at him.

---

1. This exact sentiment was also articulated recently (2007) on a poster pasted outside Bristol Railway Station in England; the caption read: "Britain accepts careful terrorists."

Žižek's reference to the film *Brassed Off* highlights this very logic: only by giving up the political struggle does one paradoxically make the political gesture par excellence.[2] The film explores the relationship between two ideologies: on the one hand there is the political: the disintegration of the old-style working class within a South Yorkshire mining community facing pit closures; on the other hand there is the "Only the music matters!" attitude of their old and dying colliery bandmaster played by Pete Postlethwaite (TS, 351). As Žižek explains, although the two initially appear opposed — music is a vain pleasure in the harsh light of economic reality — it is only when the political struggle is ceded, i.e., when the band plays purely and simply for the integrity of the music itself, that they make the political gesture par excellence: "Once the miners lose their political struggle, however, the 'Music matters' attitude, their insistence on playing and participating in a national competition, turns into a defiant symbolic gesture, a proper act of asserting fidelity to their political struggle" (TS, 351). Likewise, this book assumes the position that only by ceding the priority of secular liberalism, making instead the theological turn, can we recover the Left's political edge.

Such a standpoint is not likely to court favor with the Left, especially given the antireligious rhetoric of much of Marxism, and no more so than now, when the climate of suspicion against religion is such that any public expression of faith is likely to open one up to charges of fundamentalism. Indeed, it is possible to detect this suspicion among many of Žižek's critics. For example, Geoff Boucher asks whether or not the religious content of Žižek's work risks a form of "irrational fundamentalism,"[3] while Yannis Stavrakakis is critical of Žižek's language of faith, claiming it risks "political absolutisation."[4] Matthew Sharpe gives a more measured response, although he likewise says that Žižek's theological turn can "easily collapse into a perverse identification . . . with the mechanisms of prohibition themselves, rather than a passage beyond law," as

2. Mark Herman, *Brassed Off* (Channel Four Films, 1996).

3. Geoff Boucher, "The Law as Thing: Žižek and the Graph of Desire," in *Traversing the Fantasy: Critical Responses to Slavoj Žižek*, ed. G. Boucher, J. Glynos, and M. Sharpe (Aldershot: Ashgate, 2005), pp. 23-46, 44.

4. Yannis Stavrakakis, "The Lure of Antigone: *Aproias* of an Ethics of the Political," in *Traversing the Fantasy*, p. 44.

attested by the history of the Christian churches.[5] It is not that these critics are wrong: religious absolutism *can* lead to political absolutism; it is
that theology is only represented through these negative associations
with fundamentalism or totalitarianism. Nowhere is the study of theology urged by these writers as a creative resource for the Left. In this very
absence they expose their implicit positivism: any political-social theory
should be built only upon solid and empirical facts ascertained from the
ground up.

In *Did Somebody Say Totalitarianism?* Žižek provides a response in
advance of his critics. He warns that within the context of such debates,
the very word "fundamentalism," like totalitarianism, "far from being an
effective theoretical concept, is a kind of *stopgap:* instead of enabling us
to think, forcing us to acquire a new insight into the historical reality it
describes, it relieves us of the duty to think, or even actively *prevents* us
thinking" (DSST, 3).

The plaintive cry of "fundamentalism" silences intelligible debate,
thereby guaranteeing the hegemony of liberal secularism, dismissing the
religious critique of secularism as its obverse: intolerant madness. In
short, the suggestion of fundamentalism implies theology need not be
taken seriously. The failure of Žižek's critics to engage theology appears
to confirm this very point. This book takes the opposite stance: theology
matters.[6]

This introduction also refuses the standpoint of Ian Parker's *Slavoj
Žižek: A Critical Introduction.* Parker draws on the controversial work of
David Bakan, who in *Sigmund Freud and the Jewish Mystical Tradition*
(1958) makes the case that psychoanalysis is a secular rewriting of Judaism.[7] Freud's work was, he says, infused with the Jewish "religious, mysti-

---

5. Matthew Sharpe, *Slavoj Žižek: A Little Piece of the Real* (Aldershot: Ashgate, 2004),
p. 250.

6. Significantly the two volumes of Žižek's essays edited by Rex Butler and Scott
Stephens, *Interrogating the Real* (2005) and *Universal Exception* (2006), acknowledge the
"generosity" of the Australian Theological Foundation during the early stages of the project.

7. Criticism of Bakan's work can be found in Peter Gay, *A Godless Jew: Freud, Atheism,
and the Making of Psychoanalysis* (New Haven and London: Yale University Press, 1987), pp.
130-32; Martha Robert, *From Oedipus to Moses: Freud's Jewish Identity,* trans. Ralph
Manheim (New York: Anchor Books, 1976), pp. 171-72; Emanuel Rice, *Freud and Moses: The
Long Journey Home* (Albany: SUNY Press, 1990), p. 119.

cal and cultural tradition . . . organised through an oral tradition which is
devoted to re-readings of the Torah, the Talmud and a host of Rabbinical
commentaries," and "Lacan's work is properly psychoanalytic insofar as
it retains that link with the broad cultural tradition of secularised Judaism."[8] The problem arises for Parker because in Žižek's work, what has
formally been "subdued, mainly submerged within the broader Judaic
tradition of psychoanalysis," i.e., Christ, is given "centre-stage." In short,
Žižek is guilty of supersessionism: the "Christianising"[9] of a "Jewish science."[10] But Parker's argument fails on a number of key points. First,
Bakan's initial assumption is questionable. For example, the prominent
biographer of Freud, Peter Gay, argues that Freud, known for his ac-
knowledgment of sources, never lists the sources Bakan invents for
him.[11] Moreover, in contrast to Bakan's thesis, the argument presented
in *Moses and Monotheism* explicitly credits Jewish monotheism with the
advancement of *Geistigkeit* — an intellectual and abstract thought that
historically overcomes a magical or mystical way of thinking (SE, 23:113).
If Freud was Jewish, he was not a mystical Jew.

Second, one can hardly call the Christian thematic in Lacan's work
"submerged." He refers to the key to language by the first line of the
Christian benediction: *the name of the Father,* and the triangulation of
the real/imaginary/symbolic as the Trinity. He called Roman Catholicism the "true religion" and dedicated a number of seminars to the
topic.[12] What is perhaps more intriguing is the way Parker paints Christianity as the repressed content of Lacan, but also that which must stay
repressed, as if it should have no bearing on Lacan's work as a whole.
This seems to contravene the axioms of psychoanalysis.

Third, Parker gives no sense in which a Christian engagement with

8. Ian Parker, *Slavoj Žižek: A Critical Introduction* (London: Pluto, 2004), p. 119.
9. Parker, *Slavoj Žižek*, p. 120.
10. Parker, *Slavoj Žižek*, p. 119.
11. Gay, *A Godless Jew*, pp. 130-32.
12. Lacan, "Conference de Presse du Dr Lacan," in *Lettres de l'Ecole Freudienne* (Bulle-
tin interieur de l'Ecole Freudienne de Paris, 1974), in William Richardson, "'Like Straw':
Religion and Psychoanalysis," *The Letter: Lacanian Perspectives on Psychoanalysis* 11 (1997):
1-15, 8. See also Lacan, *Le Triomphe de Religion/Discours auc Catholiques* (Paris: Seuil,
2005).

psychoanalysis might prove beneficial. He jumps too quickly to the charge of supersessionism, putting Žižek's interest in Christianity down to a more general resurgence of Catholicism within Slovenia following the collapse of atheist Yugoslavia. The implication of this latter claim should not be overlooked. Parker is arguing that Žižek's desire to Christianize psychoanalysis is part of a Catholic and nationalist anti-Semitism, although he does not spell this out explicitly. Yet missing from his own account is any attempt to formally and philosophically explore the relation between Christianity and psychoanalysis or acknowledge the specific ways in which Žižek has elaborated Christian/Jewish relations. Neither does he explore the complex issues surrounding anti-Semitism. Yet this is precisely what Žižek's employment of Lacan's theoretical apparatus enables him to do — highlight the often paradoxical interrelations of Christianity and Judaism in ways that sit well with the argument put forward by Freud in *Moses and Monotheism.*

Parker further expresses his unease with the religious aspect of Žižek's thought when he says: "Although Žižek makes a distinction in *The Puppet and the Dwarf* between the 'perverse' ideological universe of 'really existing Christianity' and the redemptive new beginning promised by Christ that he aims to retrieve from that universe, his favourite texts are those of reactionary Catholic writers like G. K. Chesterton and C. S. Lewis."[13] In other words, although Žižek recognizes the difference between the redemptive message of Christianity and the historical — and at times less forgiving — reality of the Christian churches, he nonetheless has the audacity to read reactionary Catholics! But why does Parker use the word "reactionary" rather than "radical," other than to suggest that the work of these authors has no intrinsic merit. How does he make that judgment? Moreover, Parker incorrectly assumes that C. S. Lewis was a Catholic; Lewis was an Anglican. This alone should suggest that Žižek's interest is not simply an expression of Slovenian-Catholic nationalism, but a rich play of intellectual heritages, politically, psychoanalytically, and theologically diverse. If Žižek has a strength, it is that he is not afraid to be critical of Marxism, and in being so to find resources within theology or Christianity — as did Marx himself, who borrowed a theolog-

---

13. Parker, *Slavoj Žižek,* p. 120.

ical eschatology to ground his work. This book is written with the view that the "subdued, mainly submerged" content of Lacan should be allowed to speak, and that the current theological turn among the Left — including Alain Badiou and Peter Hallward — may be rooted in the recognition that socialism of the Left requires something more than a positivist account of the social, i.e., a bare description of the social object in all its finitude. Rather, what is needed is the creative and imaginative passion awakened through recourse to the infinite.

It can also be argued that any introduction to Žižek *has* to be theological for three reasons. First, the complex interweaving of theology, political theory, and psychology makes it difficult to read Žižek *without* taking into account the formative role theology plays, in terms of both his sources — G. K. Chesterton, Schelling, Kierkegaard — and his direct admonitions. As Scott Stephens has recently argued:

> When Žižek states unequivocally that Capital is Real, he is making a serious claim about the ontology of our global situation: the specific nature of Capital demands an appropriate form of philosophico-political activity. . . . [D]irect intervention can be transubstantiated into an expression of Capital itself. The only proper activity now is to think Capital, not as it actually exists, but theologically, at the level of its substance. This theological withdrawal, of course, repeats Marx's criticism that all economists "share the error of examining surplus-value not as such, in its pure form, but in the particular forms of profit and rent."[14]

Second, and more generally, theology has been the foremost cultural and philosophical influence in the West. For this reason, any introductory work on philosophy, politics, and psychology must take theology seriously if it is to critically engage its own presuppositions. Indeed, it is because theology has been so culturally formative that one can readily find similar questions to those posed in other areas, in which alternative an-

14. Scott Stephens, "Žižek, My Neighbour — regarding Jodi Dean's *Žižek's Politics*," *International Journal of Žižek Studies* 1 (2007); http://zizekstudies.org/index.php/ijzs/issue/view/2 (accessed August 29, 2007). See also Karl Marx, *Theories of Surplus Value*, vol. 1, ed. S. Ryazanskaya, trans. E. Burns (Moscow: Progress Publishers, 1963), p. 40.

swers or possibilities become available, answers that may give some direction in the current debates.

Thirdly, the idea that any introduction could be *un*theological presupposes that *either* there can be a neat, autonomous, and self-contained sphere of the secular *or* that god, if there is one, would remain nonetheless extrinsic and distanced from the world and hence easily accommodated to the private sphere of ineffability, remotely distanced from political concerns.

The former invokes an ahistoricism by positing a realm of secular facticity. Yet according to the theologian John Milbank, secularity was not simply "there" waiting to be discovered once "the pressure of the sacred was relaxed";[15] it was genealogically constructed through the emergent political sciences, which were in themselves already bastardized forms of theology. Concepts such as political sovereignty, autonomy, property, power, and the like emerged from a nontrinitarian theism that celebrated the absolute will of the divine, and easily translated into the monarch, and finally toward a liberal anthropology that celebrates atomistic individuals and defines individuality specifically in terms of the *will*.[16] Moreover, as Milbank further highlights, Marx tended to assert the priority of the economic base over and against the ideological superstructure of which religion was the prime example: get rid of religion and we can see how things really are. Yet as Durkheim recognized: "Society only exists through its symbolic self-representation,"[17] and so there can be no socioeconomic reality more basic than religion. Indeed, one way to read the current theological turn in French philosophy is as a growing consensus on this very point. Hence, I contend, any introduction to Žižek must necessarily engage theology.

The latter point (that were there a god, he would remain nonetheless extrinsic) is theologically dubious. As the Jesuit Henri de Lubac would say, "God is never absent from his work: he did not create and leave."[18] Rather, as Augustine understood it, the creative God is *Deus interior*

---

15. Milbank, *Theology and Social Theory,* 2nd ed. (Oxford: Blackwell, 2006), p. 8.

16. Fergus Kerr, "Simplicity Itself: Milbank's Thesis," *New Blackfriars* 861 (1992): 306-10, 306.

17. Quoted in Milbank, *Theology and Social Theory,* p. 67.

18. Henri de Lubac, *The Mystery of the Supernatural* (New York: Crossroad, 1998), p. 20.

intimo meo, "the God who is more interior to me than I am myself."[19] That is to say, the realm of the supernatural is not some extra appendage that occasionally bursts through in a punctilious fashion — the predominant model underpinning evangelism; the world and matter are given as *already* supernatural in ways that paradoxically transcend the sphere of a natural order. And because the social is now given as the sphere of religion, religion becomes especially concerned with the social; or rather, theology is recognized as psychosocial theory.

Beyond that, this book has three other aims in mind. First, to provide a general and intelligible introduction to the work of Žižek. For example, careful consideration is given to the exposition of onto-theology, metaphysics, traversing the fantasy, and other concepts. To that end, this book assumes little prior knowledge on the part of the reader. In presenting Žižek, I have also been careful to relate his work back to Lacan and the clinical practice of psychoanalysis. This may seem a rather obvious move; after all, Žižek is a self-declared Lacanian, and any introduction therefore requires grounding in Lacan. Yet arguably Žižek's success has been in translating the texts of Lacan that are renowned for their theoretical complexity into popular media such as the films of Alfred Hitchcock or advertisements; or transposing his work into the philosophical idiom of German idealism. Yet what this can miss is the historical and practical experience of psychoanalysis out of which these concepts initially emerged, and this can be enormously helpful in understanding the concepts, even if only initially to dispel some of the prejudice surrounding them. Lacan's account of feminine sexuality provides a good example of this. It is easy to sound out his claim "that the woman does not exist" for treating woman as a lack, writing her out to ensure masculine domination. But arguably the very critical gesture occurs when one first asks what clinical problem Lacan initially addressed, and is able thereafter to respond in this regard. In the above case, the problem arose because men were only too *good* at describing women; there was no lack of men offering in advance a diagnosis of the feminine subject before she had entered the clinic, presupposing the nature of feminine sexuality along the lines of castration (i.e., masculinity). The very critical gesture there-

---

19. Lubac, *Mystery of the Supernatural*, p. 78.

fore lies in rethinking the formulae from the question addressed: How should the clinic, and by extension wider social relations, address that problem?

Second, this book extends the application of Lacan to theology in the manner of Žižek. For example, in chapter 3 I explore how the formulae of sexuation apply to Aquinas and the sacraments to provide imaginative interpretations.

Third, this introduction provides a comprehensive account of the theology and theological examples within Žižek's work, while traversing politics and psychology, highlighting explicitly the various ways in which Žižek's theology directly informs his politics, or the point that political allusions slip into theological ones. In this way I hope this book will be of special interest to students of religious studies, and students of politics or philosophy with an interest in theology. The rest of this introduction provides a general introduction to Žižek and Lacan, and the plan of the book.

Lacan

Looming behind Žižek is the theoretical brilliance of Jacques-Marie Lacan (1901-81), the French psychoanalyst who spearheaded the "return to Freud" movement in the latter half of the twentieth century. Despite the complexity of his thought, the general thrust of his endeavor is easy to grasp (unlike Freud, whose simple prose belies the complexity). Lacan was the first psychoanalyst to read Freud from the perspective of structural linguistics. In other words, it is as if everything Freud said was true (e.g., the Oedipus complex, castration, the unconscious, and so on), only Freud was *really* talking about language. For example, the Oedipus complex is not so much about the biological desire for the mother and murderous intent toward the father; rather, it tells the story about how we learn to substitute the body of the mother for language by accepting the master signifier: the phallus (i.e., lack), as the key that unlocks the creativity of language as a whole. Equally, castration ceases to be a story about a child's fear of losing (or in the case of a girl, having already lost) the biological penis; rather it refers to the effect language has upon the speaking subject; the way that, however much one says, there is always an element of meaning that evades us (the symbolic phallus). And finally, the unconscious is not a dark receptacle buried deep within in which all one's repressed content resides. Rather, it is like a language, out there, hidden in full view within the very words one uses. The unconscious operates as a thief who hides a diamond in a chandelier.

In developing Freud's work, Lacan came up with a model to rival Freud's id, ego, and superego: the real, imaginary, and symbolic. When we enter the cultural sociosymbolic world, there is a part that refuses to be entertained,[20] an excess or "accursed share" that is experienced as the "missed encounter" (SXI, 55), what Lacan calls the real *(réel)*. The real is that inaccessible aspect that haunts psychic life: "the essential object which isn't an object any longer, but this something faced with which all words cease and all categories fail, the object of anxiety *par excellence*" (SII, 164). Hence the real corresponds to *trauma,* from the Greek τραῦμα, to wound or pierce:[21] an encounter with the real is an encounter with the point where the coherency of a moment is pierced and the symbolic support of one's identity begins to give way (SXI, 55); hence the real is closely associated with death and the death drive. In the development of his thought, Lacan also refers to the real in terms of *the Thing (das Ding)*. In this way he evokes resonances with Kant's *noumenon,*[22] an object not discernible to sensible intuition, discernible only in terms of the effects it produces. Lacan differs from Kant to the extent that the real is not the transcendental support of the subject, as it is for Kant, but the immanent inertia of the subject that evades symbolization (SIII, 13). *Das Ding* also recalls Heidegger's essay of the same name. Here, *das Ding* plays the part of the constitutive void around which being coalesces. Finally, the real is associated with the mother because it is the mother from whom the child must principally separate, substituting her body for the body of law; i.e., the symbolic (SVII, 67).

The imaginary refers to the sense of wholeness the child first per-

20. Literally, it is barred from entertainment, i.e., enjoyment.

21. Jean Laplanche and Jean-Bertrand Pontalis, *The Language of Psychoanalysis,* trans. D. Nicholson-Smith (London: Karnac Books, 1988), pp. 465-69.

22. Immanuel Kant, *Critique of Pure Reason,* trans. J. M. D. Meiklejohn (London: Everyman, 1993), p. 211.

ceives in the mirror at around six months to eighteen months (É, 75-81/ 93-100). Contrary to the child's embodied experience — undeveloped motor skills and the like — the mirror image seems to confer upon the child the promise of a unified wholeness separate from the mother. As Lacan says, in its initial stages a child has little coordination over its body; however, in the mirror "the sight alone of the whole form of the human body gives the subject an imaginary mastery over his body, one which is premature in relation to a real mastery" (SI, 79). The mirror image copies exactly every given action. The imaginary order is characterized by dyadic relationships established between the specular image (i.e., the image of one's body) and his ego. Yet the imaginary image is a false image, and so while it comes to stand for the unity and sameness conferred by a narcissistic relation, it ends up in alienation and aggression.

The symbolic refers to the realm of law (e.g., language) that governs all social relations, replacing the body of the mother. Yet the symbolic introduces a split *(Spaltung)* into the subject, opening up a gap between their empirical being and their symbolic status; Lacan refers to this distinction in terms of the subject of the enunciation (the empirical being that speaks) and the subject of the statement (the words spoken). The symbolic introduces a cut, alienating the subject in himself as he is from his mother. Entering the symbolic therefore entails giving up the unity offered by imaginary identifications for an all-encompassing structure that is devoid of any fixed relations, a linguistic barrier or "wall of language" (SII, 244) behind which stands the inaccessible real of experience.

Theorist of the *Real*

Although ostensibly a mouthpiece for Lacan, applying the master to innovative areas of culture and politics, Žižek engages him in a particular way. Žižek focuses on what he deems Lacan's so-called "third period" (SOI, 133), when the emphasis in his teaching shifted from an interest in symbolic structures and our place within them, to the real of experience. It was during this period that Lacan says: "no praxis is more orientated towards that which, at the heart of experience, is the kernel of the real than psychoanalysis" (SXI, 53). In this regard Žižek has helped cultivate a more nuanced understanding of this difficult concept, shifting the emphasis away from the real as inaccessible support of reality to the way we actually encounter it, albeit in a way that preserves its negative status:

> the Real is impossible but it is not simply impossible in the sense of a failed encounter. It is also impossible in the sense that it is a traumatic encounter that *does* happen but which we are unable to confront. And one of the strategies used to avoid confronting it is precisely that of positing it as this indefinite ideal which is eternally postponed. One aspect of the real is that it's impossible, but the other aspect is that it happens but is impossible to sustain, impossible to integrate. And this second aspect, I think, is more and more crucial. (C, 71)

This distinction is important for highlighting the shift Žižek introduces in the reception of Lacan. Prior to Žižek, the tendency was to read Lacan in the light of Derrida or post-structuralism, where the emphasis falls on difference, alterity, and undecidability, a project indebted in many ways to Heidegger's account of ontological difference. However, as James Smith argues, the problem arises because from the perspective of politics, undecidability can easily come to mean "*indecision,* a kind of paralysis in the face of the power to decide,"[23] a stammering apophaticism in the political arena serving to undermine the possibility of engaged critical acts. By contrast, Žižek argues that the real *can happen;* in other words, one *can* act. By confronting the real of experience, one can bring the entire sociosymbolic into question, in such a way as to reconfigure it in its entirety, so future action, political or otherwise, need not be circumscribed by neurotic repetition but can embrace imaginative possibilities.

Žižek often describes this act as requiring a "suspension of the symbolic," an allusion to Kierkegaard's "suspension of the ethical" (see chapter 1); a radical moment of transition in which one passes from reason to faith, leaving behind all symbolic supports through commitment to God. In doing so Žižek makes the point that a political act requires risk, because it is the very structure that determines what can be known that is

23. James Smith, *Jacques Derrida: Live Theory* (New York and London: Continuum, 2005), p. 82.

at stake. There is something of Rousseau in this. If people act according to their own self-interests, they inevitably consult the same predictable desires; but when people make decisions with recourse to the general will, i.e., not out of self-interest, their actions require a certain risk because they will be unpredictable and therefore free.[24] Hence, when Žižek makes the point that politics is a matter of *faith,* he does not mean in the usual liberal sense of the term — a matter of personal choice or a subjective belief — but what Kierkegaard calls the passion of inwardness, i.e., an absolute commitment in which one risks everything for the unknown, because only where there is risk, is there passion, and as Kierkegaard says, risk raises the "passion as high as possible."[25]

Lacan and Religion

Given the role of religion in Žižek's work, it is helpful to know something of Lacan's relation to it. Lacan typically affirms Freud's thesis set out in *Future of an Illusion* that religion is a defense, a form of neurosis to protect us against harsh reality: "if death itself is not something spontaneous but the violent act of an evil Will, if everywhere in nature there are Beings around us of a kind that we know in our society, then we can breathe freely" (SE, 21:16-17), or as Lacan says: "Religion in all its forms consists of avoiding this emptiness" (SVII, 130) upon which life is predicated. However, Lacan is more skeptical than Freud about Freud's claim that science will replace religion (SE, 21:56): "[religion and psychoanalysis] are not very amicable. In sum, it is either one or the other. If religion triumphs as is most probable — I speak of the true religion and there is only one which is true [i.e., Roman Catholicism] — if religion triumphs, this will be the sign that psychoanalysis has failed."[26] Why does Lacan think religion will triumph over psychoanalysis? Because religion is "capable of giving a meaning, one can say, to anything at all — a meaning to

24. J. S. McClelland, *A History of Western Political Thought* (London and New York: Routledge, 1996), p. 262.

25. S. Kierkegaard, *Concluding Unscientific Postscript,* vol. 1, trans. H. Hong and E. Hong (Princeton: Princeton University Press, 1992), p. 385.

26. Richardson, "Like Straw," pp. 8-9.

human life for example."[27] Yet meaning implies unity, and the singular feature of the unconscious is discontinuity, a forgotten word, a bungled action, or a slip of the tongue; what Freud called the parapraxis.[28]

Little wonder then that Lacan maintained a critical distance from religion: to posit God as the *causa sui* risks "drowning" life in meaning.[29] It would, as William Richardson says, close the chain of signification in upon a center that would hold the signifier and signified together to become the "absolute foundation of meaning."[30] This is why Lacan says the true formula of atheism is not God is dead, but *"God is unconscious"* (SXI, 59); in other words, to affirm the death of God is to affirm the slippage of meaning and the role of unconscious desire in shaping our actions; it is to affirm that we find our gods too easily in wholesome answers.

Mario Beira has argued that Lacan shares a deep affinity with Christianity, the product of an unresolved trauma centered upon what Lacan calls the *Name-of-the-Father* (É, 230/278) — the basis of symbolic function, the creative principle that unlocks language's potential as a whole.[31] According to Beira, Lacan's unconscious desire was shaped by a key event concerning the father: he was the only one of his three siblings not to have been born on Christmas Day, unable, as it were, to assume the position of the Christ child for the father.[32] No wonder he positioned himself with regard to Freud the way he did, ensuring, in a parody of Saint John, that "No one comes to the father [Freud] except through me" (John 14:6). Moreover, by shortening his name from Jacques-Marie to Jacques — Lacan had been given the name Marie in honor of the Virgin Mary, the patron saint of the family vinegar trade[33] — he was able to cut the umbilical cord to the Madonna and assume the position of Christ, an

27. Richardson, "Like Straw," p. 9.

28. "Act whose explicit goal is not attained; instead this goal turns out to have been replaced by another one." Laplanche and Pontalis, *The Language of Psychoanalysis*, p. 300.

29. Richardson, "Like Straw," p. 12.

30. Richardson, "Like Straw," p. 11.

31. Mario Beira, "Lacan, Psio-análisis y el Dios de Moisés," in *Lacan en Estados Unidos*, ed. Donna Bentolila-Lopez (Rosario, Argentina: Homo Sapiens, 1989), pp. 121-38.

32. Elisabeth Roudinesco, *Jacques Lacan*, trans. Barbara Bray (London: Polity, 1999), p. 460.

33. Shuli Barzilai, *Lacan and the Matter of Origins* (Stanford: Stanford University Press, 1999), p. 151.

exiled prophet to redeem his Moses (Freud) against a Jewish establishment that would ultimately sacrifice him by expelling him from the body Freud created: the International Psychoanalytical Association.

Moreover, in a now famous incident recorded by the historian of French psychoanalysis Elisabeth Roudinesco, Lacan sent a letter to his brother, Marc-François, a Benedictine monk, asking him to intercede on his behalf to obtain an audience with Pope Pius XII, thereby doing "homage to our common Father."[34] According to Roudinesco, Lacan was not renouncing atheism as such. He knew that reading Freud from a philosophical and nonbiological point of view would attract Catholics who had previously found Freud's materialism too reductionist of religion.[35] But this merely begs the question, why attract the Catholics in the first place?

Elsewhere Roudinesco has been quick to point out that Lacan made similar attempts to secure a meeting with Mao Zedong.[36] Her argument is that given the powerful political presence of the psychoanalytic institution to which Lacan fell foul, he would call upon the two other most powerful institutions for support; hence his gesture was not so much about bringing psychoanalysis closer to Catholicism, but of bringing the Catholics, and likewise the communists, closer to himself. But can one so easily brush off the profound theological resonances within his work as a matter of political expediency?

Lacan's elder brother, Marc-François, paints a different picture. He describes Lacan as having had a "very deep personal Christian culture" during his early studies, ensuring for example that his children were baptized.[37] And his doctoral thesis of 1932 was initially dedicated to his brother with the words: "To the Reverend Father Marc-François Lacan, Benedictine of the Congregation of France, my brother in religion," although it was changed in the reprint.[38]

34. Roudinesco, *Jacques Lacan*, p. 205.

35. Roudinesco, *Jacques Lacan*, p. 205.

36. Roudinesco, "Psychoanalysis and Homosexuality: Reflections on the Perverse Desire, Insult and the Paternal Function," *Journal of European Psychoanalysis*, no. 15 (Fall/Winter 2002); www.psychomedia.it/jep/number15/roudinesco.htm (accessed August 19, 2007).

37. Paul Roazen, "Lacan's First Disciple," *Journal of Religious Health* 4 (1996): 321-36, 324.

38. Roazen, "Lacan's First Disciple," p. 328.

Moreover, we learn in "Science and Truth" (É, 726-46), which was written between 1965 and 1966, something of his Catholicism. Here, in the words of Miller, Lacan "makes a sarcastic critique of Ecumenism which was de rigueur in the Catholic Church at the time and was part of *aggiornamento*."[39] From this we learn two things. First, Lacan was publicly and critically engaging with the Catholic debates surrounding Vatican II. Second, contrary to his place in the bosom of left-wing radicals, Lacan was a deeply conservative Catholic who resisted the liberal tendency to efface the details of one's belief in favor of some common denominator, a move he referred to as "feebleminded" (É, 742/874).

Finally, it seems Lacan was drawn from his early days to seek out the company of Catholics, many of whom would become his closest allies during his troubles with the French psychoanalytic community, including the analysts François Dolto and François Roustang and the Jesuits Denis Vasse and Father Louis Beirnaert. Perhaps, then, a properly theological reading need not imply an aberration of Lacan's work, but the hidden telos of his work, hidden in full view in the dedication of his doctoral thesis to his brother.

The Gospel

If Lacan implicitly positions himself as Christ, Žižek has no compunction in openly assuming the position of apostle: "Deep down I am very conservative; I just play at this subversive stuff. My most secret dream is to write an old-fashioned, multivolume theological tract on Lacanian theory in the style of Aquinas. I would examine each of Lacan's theories in a completely dogmatic way, considering the arguments for and against each statement and then offering a commentary. I would be happiest if I could be a monk in my cell, with nothing to do but write my Summa Lacaniana."[40]

39. Jacques-Alain Miller, "The Inexistent Seminar," *Psychoanalytic Notebooks* 15 (2005): 9-42, 26.

40. Žižek, in Robert Boyton, "Enjoy Your Žižek: An Excitable Slovenian Philosopher Examines the Obscene Practices of Everyday Life, Including His Own," *Linguafranca* 26 (March 2001); http://www.lacan.com/Žižek-enjoy.htm (accessed August 22, 2007).

As Claudia Breger notes, the usual democratically inclined modern reader will likely find this approach counterintuitive, because central to the assumption of modernity is an ability to use reason for oneself, free from the restraints of tradition. *Sapere Aude!* Yet Žižek eschews the objective/critical practice of reading Lacan; so, for example, he does not follow Lacan because Lacan provides a more intelligent and convincing interpretation of Freud than any other interpreter. Lacan assumes his position in Žižek's work as the Teacher whose texts are accorded the status of Holy Scripture, and his task is to provide a commentary, making the link between Lacan's personal authority and the doctrine.[41]

Indeed, Žižek explicitly relates this model of authority to Kierkegaard's distinction between the life of the genius and the life of the apostle. According to Kierkegaard, genius is what it is of itself, it is "immediateness (*ingenium*, that which is inborn)."[42] Genius is therefore qualified naturally; i.e., it is born. But it is otherwise with the apostle. What the apostle brings is from outside. The apostle is not responsible for the content of the message; he merely has to convey it correctly. Unlike the genius, he has no authority over the message that corresponds to any intrinsic merit by that individual (in the way a musical genius may be attributed authority in musical matters); there is no link between the apostle's personal identity and the message. The apostle becomes, as Žižek says, merely a support and is what he is by "divine authority" (EYS, 94-95).[43]

On that basis, Žižek's entire oeuvre may be said to repeat the scandal of Christianity. In Christianity truth is not innately and eternally given but latent, waiting to be discovered (what Kierkegaard called paganism).[44] Christianity makes the claim that the truth has been revealed through a particular and contingent event: the incarnation. Likewise the scandal of Žižek's work is his failure to adopt the position of the objective rational critic, maintaining instead an uncritical fidelity to Lacan's

41. Claudia Breger, "The Leader's Two Bodies: Slavo Žižek's Postmodern Political Theology," *Diacritics* 31, no. 1 (2001): 73-90, 75-76.
42. Kierkegaard, "On the Difference between a Genius and an Apostle," in *The Present Age,* trans. Alexander Dru (London: Fontana, 1962), pp. 101-27, 106.
43. Kierkegaard, "On the Difference," p. 105.
44. Kierkegaard, *Concluding Unscientific Postscript,* pp. 243-44.

framework of discussion. Breger is right, therefore, in describing his work not so much as criticism but as "exegesis."

Scott Stephens has also commented on Žižek's secret Thomistic dream. He initially suggests that despite Žižek's engagement with imminent topics such as Iraq, Palestine, or the recent Paris riots, his writing "is deeply solipsistic and unperturbed by external phenomena,"[45] concerned mainly to articulate Lacanian theory. It is in this sense that his work is said to resemble those sprawling medieval theological tracts, such as Aquinas's *Summa,* for whom the demand to be relevant, to "have something to say" to the current situation, was inconsequential compared to the pursuit of "the Thing itself," i.e., the Lacanian real.[46]

However, in an astute turn, Stephens refers to the Swiss theologian Karl Barth, who, writing in 1933, declared: "I endeavour to carry on theology, and only theology, now as previously, and as if nothing had happened . . . something like the chanting of the hours by the Benedictines near by in the *Maria Laach,* which goes on undoubtedly without break or interruption, pursuing the even tenor of its way even in the Third *Reich.*"[47] Scott's argument is that "just as Barth's defiant restatement of the dogmatic tradition constituted one of the most effective protests against the idolatry of National Socialism, so too it is at the very point of Žižek's theoretical withdrawal from, and even indifference toward, the demand to *respond* to certain exigencies that we discover his importance for politics — and indeed, for political theology — today."[48] That is to say, the importance of his work may lie less in *what* is said than in the *way* it is said or the *"form* of his work,"[49] maintaining as it does a dogmatic devotion to Lacan in an age where the reign of the enlightened and self-idolatrous individual is sovereign.

45. Stephens, "Žižek, My Neighbour."
46. Stephens, "Žižek, My Neighbour."
47. Karl Barth, *Theological Existence To-day: A Plea for Theological Freedom,* trans. R. B. Hoyle (London: Hodder and Stoughton, 1933), p. 9, in Stephens, "Žižek, My Neighbour."
48. Stephens, "Žižek, My Neighbour."
49. Stephens, "Žižek, My Neighbour."

Outline of the Book

The outline of the book is as follows. In chapter 1, "God, Dereliction, and Violence," I provide a comprehensive and systematic overview of Žižek's theology. I center my exposition on Žižek's repeated reference to Christ's cry of dereliction upon the cross. I show how this serves as the basis for a postmetaphysical theology, as well as accounts for the relation between God and the structure of subjectivity. Heidegger, Lacan, Schelling, and Kierkegaard are all introduced to this end. I then explore the impact of Žižek's theology of abandonment on the concept of atonement as it relates to both theology and psychoanalysis. To critically engage Žižek's theology, I employ the work of René Girard, whose theory of the scapegoat highlights the radical difference between the violence of sacrifice and the peace of Christianity. My argument is as follows. On the one hand, Žižek's theology is predicated upon its revolutionary nature: Christ's death on the cross — while taking the form of a sacrifice — breaks with sacrificial logic because what dies is the very guarantor of such a system (i.e., God). Yet on the other hand, his entire theoretical apparatus is predicated upon such a sacrificial system, leaving the violence of sacrifice as the horizon of the political. Said otherwise, Žižek remains locked into the very system he is critical of. I conclude by questioning whether abandonment on the cross was really the final word, as Žižek suggests.

In chapter 2, "Belief before Belief," I explore Marx's theory of ideology and its development via Althusser and Žižek. Žižek traces the original critique of ideology to the religious figure Job, whose suffering is said to foreshadow Christ's. In this way he makes the connection between the critique of ideology and the religious critique of metaphysics. However, I take up Matthew Sharpe's skepticism regarding the possibility of Žižek's work *sustaining* an ideological critique. Drawing on the work of Conor Cunningham, I highlight the nihilism that underpins Žižek's ontology. However, rather than simply oppose nihilism with theology, I show the overlap between Cunnigham's theological critique of nihilism and Žižek's critique of onto-theology. By giving a more theologically grounded critique of ideology, I suggest a reading of Žižek that is able to overcome the very problem identified by Sharpe: a sustainable and progressive socialism.

In chapter 3, "Why the Political Act Must Necessarily Adopt the Form of the Religious Act," I explore in some depth Žižek's concept of the political act, an act that has the character of an event, challenging the very coordinates of the system rather than coordinates within the system. In this regard I highlight Žižek's debt to Alain Badiou's work on Saint Paul, the "truth process," and the religious dimension to the political act. Taking into account Žižek's criticism of Badiou, I also bring John Milbank's theological critique to bear upon Žižek: Žižek's work sustains an ontology of revolution but not the progressive path toward socialism; for this a return of a different kind is required. I develop Milbank's criticism in the light of the *ressourcement* theologians, a group of French Jesuits and Dominicans who spearheaded a return to the patristic sources of theology from the 1930s to the 1960s. However, this is no mere instance of opposing one to the other. My claim is that their initial "return" had a decisive influence on Lacan's *return-to-Freud;* by "returning to the return" and mining the theological underpinnings of Lacan's work, I move beyond the impasse in Žižek's work. Finally, I respond to Žižek's claim that the political act requires an ahistorical kernel that proves constitutive of genuine historical — and hence political — change. Bringing Kierkegaard into the debate, I argue that the incarnation is the ahistorical kernel by which history is constituted par excellence, and hence Christianity the condition of the political act.

In chapter 4, "Sexual Difference and Non-All *(Pas-tout),*" I explore Žižek's development of Lacan's formulae of sexuation as they relate to the metaphysical and postmetaphysical standpoint. I highlight the relation Žižek establishes between the logic of femininity and the critique of metaphysics; as well as the relation he plots between Judaism and masculinity, feminism and Christianity. I then bring him into dialogue with Tina Beattie to suggest that he is best read as a Catholic feminist. What is at stake for much contemporary Catholic feminism like Beattie's is a recovery of the female body, which has been traditionally sacrificed as the condition of a male hierarchy. In turn, it is understood that this order is supported by onto-theology. In this regard, Žižek's critique of metaphysics opens the way toward the recovery of the female body. However, as I argue, the material body is precisely the thing that disappears out of Žižek's theology, displaced in favor of linguistic idealism. By contrast, it is only by recourse to the divine that the possibility of the material body reappears.

Finally, by reintroducing Girard into the equation, I highlight the link between masculinity, onto-theology, and violence. By linking the feminist critic to the critique of violence, I submit that the recovery of the female body within Catholicism would not so much add to an existing structure as change fundamentally the nature of the structure, and hence constitute the political act par excellence.

One of Lacan's distinctive contributions to psychoanalysis has been to deepen the analysis of *jouissance,* or enjoyment. In the final chapter, "Enjoy Your Religion," I outline and apply Žižek's work on enjoyment as it relates to theology and religious studies. Particular attention is given to the role of law, and the superego command to enjoy, and whether or not our efforts to enjoy beyond the law end up confirming us as subjects of law. I explore what this might mean in the interreligious context; how does the economy of enjoyment give rise to racist tendencies, and in particular anti-Semitism? I then explore the relation of *jouissance* to anxiety in the work of Lacan through his reading of the *Akeidah,* bringing Žižek back into critical dialogue before posing an alternative reading of Lacan.

CHAPTER I

God, Dereliction, and Violence

My aim in this chapter is twofold. First, I provide a comprehensive and systematic overview of Žižek's theology. Secondly I critically engage his theology with a view to his project as a whole. I do this through the twin themes of dereliction and violence. Regarding the former, I argue that Žižek's theology takes as its principal motif Christ's cry of dereliction or abandonment on the cross: "My God, my God, why hast thou forsaken me?" (Mark 15:34/Matt. 27:46). This becomes the basis for a post-metaphysical theology (i.e., a materialist theology). While sympathetic to aspects of it, I am critical of the link he makes between the act of dereliction and violence. To this end I introduce the work of René Girard, whom Žižek himself draws upon. I argue, first of all, that Žižek's work is not representative of the theology it draws upon, precisely to the extent that it is predicated upon violence; second, Žižek's sanctification of violence undermines what is truly revolutionary (i.e., *very critical*) within Christianity: its outright refusal of violence, and hence the possibility of a truly political act.

The Cry of Dereliction: Overcoming Metaphysics

The basis of Žižek's theology is to be found in his repeated reference to Christ's cry of dereliction on the cross (OB, 106-51; PD, 171; PV, 106; FTKN, liii). This theological shift is in marked contrast to Freud. Freud set in opposition to religion his own science of psychoanalysis. Žižek follows

Lacan, who opposed psychoanalysis to science itself, arguing that the latter remained within the orbit of "theism."[1] In other words, Lacan claimed that science, unlike psychoanalysis, was still *too* religious. What Lacan had in mind was the way science often and implicitly depends upon a notion of a big Other — be it God, Spirit, or Nature — that has a preexisting plan of the cosmos that it is the scientist's task to discover.[2] Consider, for example, Stephen Hawking's question "Does God play dice?" or more generally the claim that science helps us uncover nature's secrets. This big Other or *subject supposed to know* anticipates all our knowing such that in the end all learning is but a rediscovery of what is already known in the mind of the creator. Said otherwise, the *subject supposed to know* acts in terms of a fundamental deadlock, securing the subject, nature, or the universe as a whole, such that if it were to be unlocked, all other terms in the field of reference would lose their meaning. Lacan often refers to the way Descartes uses this Other — God — to guarantee the truth of his scientific starting point:[3] "is not the sense of what Pascal called the 'God of philosophy' — from this reference to the Other so essential in Descartes, and which allowed us to start from it in order to secure our first step."[4] In his opposition to science, Lacan took it to be the task of psychoanalysis to put into question this big Other.[5]

The overtones of Heidegger's project are striking, in particular his criticism that metaphysics was essentially onto-theology:[6] God was

1. *The Seminar of Jacques Lacan, XV: The Psychoanalytic Act* (1967-1968), trans. C. Gallagher, unpublished, session X, 21.02.68, p. 4.

2. Cormac Gallagher, "A Reading of *The Psychoanalytic Act* (1967-1968)," *The Letter: Lacanian Perspectives on Psychoanalysis*, 2000, pp. 1-22.

3. Gallagher, "A Reading," p. 8.

4. *The Seminar of Jacques Lacan: The Logic of Phantasy* (1966-1967), trans. Cormac Gallagher, unpublished, session IX, 25.01.67, p. 3.

5. "What is stated from a science never puts in question what it was before the knowledge emerged. Who knew it?" *The Seminar of Jacques Lacan, XV*, session X, 21.02.68, p. 4.

6. Kant first used the term to describe the branch of natural theology that employed the ontological argument as proof of God's existence, in Immanuel Kant, *Critique of Pure Reason*, trans. J. M. D. Meiklejohn (London: Everyman, 1993), A632/B660. See also John Marenbon, "Aquinas, Radical Orthodoxy and the Importance of Truth," in *Deconstructing Radical Orthodoxy: Postmodern Theology, Rhetoric, and Truth*, ed. W. Hankey and D. Hedley (Aldershot: Ashgate, 2005), pp. 49-64, 55.

translated into the first principle, Being, the *causa sui,* who sustains being as a whole.[7] From the perspective of theology, God's mystery is reduced to the first cause in the chain of being; meanwhile philosophy is reduced to epistemology: what we can know concerning this first cause. By bringing Heidegger's critique to bear upon psychoanalysis, Lacan aimed to challenge the metaphysical structures that sustain subjectivity by challenging the Other as its locus of support.[8] This is the meaning of Lacan's claim: "there is no Other of the other."[9]

Lacan can also be seen to repeat the sentiments of Nietzsche's madman: "Where is God . . . , I'll tell you! *We have killed him* — you and I! We are all his murderers. But how did we do this? How were we able to drink up the sea? Who gave us the sponge to wipe away the entire horizon? What were we doing when we unchained this earth from its sun?"[10]

One could say that Lacanian analysis starts from the assumption of Nietzsche: *God is dead.* Through the art of speaking it brings into question the transcendental moorings to which we gain meaning in our lives. Lacan, however, is less convinced than Nietzsche that we have "killed God." He argues that "this Other which is precisely the God of the philosophers is not so easy to eliminate as people believe. Since in reality, it undoubtedly remains stable at the horizon, in any case, of all our thoughts."[11] In other words, the opposite of metaphysics is not the corporeal so much as psychosis, because without some minimal level of

---

7. Lacan's relation to Heidegger has been well documented in Elisabeth Roudinesco, *Jacques Lacan,* trans. Barbara Bray (London: Polity, 1999), pp. 219-31. According to Roudinesco, Lacan went to great lengths to first meet with Heidegger, gaining permission to translate Heidegger's "Logos" for the first issue of *La Psychanalyse,* a journal representative of the Société Française de Psychanalyse.

8. See William Richardson, "Psychoanalysis and the Being-question," in *Psychiatry and the Humanities: Interpreting Lacan,* vol. 6, ed. J. Smith and W. Kerrigan (London: Yale University Press, 1983), pp. 139-60.

9. Cormac Gallagher, "Overview of the Psychoanalytic Act," *The Letter: Lacanian Perspectives on Psychoanalysis,* 2000, pp. 104-14, 106.

10. F. Nietzsche, *The Gay Science,* trans. J. Nauckhoff (Cambridge: Cambridge University Press, 2001), pp. 119-20.

11. *The Seminar of Jacques Lacan, XVI: From the Other to the Other* (1968-1969), trans. C. Gallagher, unpublished, session XXII, 4.06.69, p. 3.

stability, one loses one's grip on meaning. Nonetheless, he takes it as the task of psychoanalysis to provide the "sponge," i.e., to develop the clinical tools with which to bring into question that very horizon.

What is at issue for Lacan, then, is not so much being reconciled to castration à la Freud, i.e., recognizing that we cannot be the object of desire for the mother, but rather, through an anxiety-provoking encounter with immanence, we come to recognize the nonexistence of the Other. That is to say, we come to accept that there is no external legislative authority that secures the system as a whole: the big Other through which we organize desire does not actually exist. In other words, Lacan invites us to affirm the world as sufficient unto itself and hence, as the Web site Larval Subjects puts it, we need not "refer to anything outside of the world to explain the world such as forms, essences, or God: the world contains its own principles of genesis."[12]

To clarify the above, the following point may be made regarding immanence. To speak of immanence in this way is to speak of relations, and whether in our dealings we primarily relate *to* something, remaining distinct as subject (i.e., relations of transcendence), or *in* something (i.e., immanent relations). To affirm the latter is to affirm the "alreadyness" from which we speak; that we are already always begun; what Heidegger referred to as the "givenness" of Dasein.[13]

Returning to Žižek, Christ's cry of dereliction interpreted through Lacan may initially be defined in terms of the "overcoming" of metaphysics, i.e., an acceptance by Christ concerning the death of the big Other. In other words, Christ was the first to "end metaphysics," signaled by both his cry of abandonment and his ultimate death, hence "in the experience of the death of God, we stumble upon the fact that the big Other doesn't exist [*l'Autre n'existe pas*]" (ME, 42).

12. http://larval-subjects.blogspot.com/2006_01_larval-subjects_archive.html (accessed January 12, 2007).

13. This account is indebted to Larval Subjects; http://larval-subjects.blogspot.com/2006_01_larval-subjects_archive.html (accessed January 12, 2007).

God's Self-Dereliction: Schelling

In Žižek's work, Christ's cry of dereliction mirrors God's own self-dereliction in the constitutive moment of creation. This is the basis of Žižek's remarkable reading of Friedrich Schelling's *Ages of the World* (1813) where Schelling provides an equally remarkable mythical, poetic, and metaphysical account of the rational and created order as it emerges from the Absolute. As with Žižek's reading of Hegel and Kant, he has an aim in mind: "the core of my entire work is the endeavour to use Lacan as the privileged intellectual tool to re-actualise German Idealism" (ZR, ix). In other words, he reads Schelling as a forerunner to Lacan.[14] In particular, he argues that Schelling's account of the passage from chaos to creation anticipates Lacan's account of the passage from the real to the symbolic, i.e., the process of becoming a subject; so we can read Schelling's account of the Absolute in anticipation of the modern Lacanian subject.

Schelling belonged to a generation of dialectical German theologians including Jakob Böhme (1575-1624), Franz von Baader (1765-1841), and Hegel (1770-1831). Considered dialectical thinkers, they were also theosophers in the medieval sense of the word: they attempted to understand the wisdom of God through a natural theology. They strove to think through the transition from God's illimitableness to the self-imposed limitation of contingent and material reality, and the paradoxes raised thereby. Conceived in Platonic terms, as Schelling himself did, how did the eternally perfect ideas generate by themselves an extra-ideal and corruptible reality? How did God arrive at material creation?[15]

According to Schelling — or rather, Žižek's paraphrasing of Schelling — in arriving at creation there were three distinct operations on the part of the Absolute — what Schelling called *the ages of the world*. In the first instance, prior to any material ground *(Grund)*, there is only an abyss *(Ungrund)* of "absolute indifference *qua* the abyss of pure Freedom that is

---

14. Here Žižek is in good company with Freud, who drew on Schelling for his account of *Unheimlich*: "*Unheimlich* is the name for everything that ought to have remained secret and hidden but has come to light" (SE, 17:224).

15. Edward Beach, *The Potencies of God(s): Schelling's Philosophy of Mythology* (Albany: SUNY Press, 1994), p. 97.

not yet the predicate-property of some Subject, but rather designates a pure impersonal Willing *(Wollen)* that wills nothing" (ZR, 258). That is to say, in the beginning God is "pure Nothingness that rejoices in its non-being" (ZR, 258). The problem arises, however, because God is pure potential, experienced as spiritual hunger or longing; but because the longing cannot find satisfaction, it becomes a fierce and chaotic fire that turns in upon itself and consumes itself.

In this, the second moment, the Absolute qua abyss of freedom *contracts,* i.e., it condenses or compresses, withdrawing into itself (AF, 16). As Žižek says, "the blissful peace of primordial freedom changes into pure contraction, into the divine vortex of 'divine madness' that threatens to swallow everything into the highest affirmation of God's egoism which tolerates nothing outside of itself" (ZR, 258). In other words, God had to negate his own essence and freedom. Following the remarkable work of Agata Bielik-Robson,[16] I suggest that one might find a parallel for the notion of "contraction" precipitating creation in the Jewish mystical tradition of Kabbalah. Kabbalists who sought to maintain the absolute difference between the fallen world and God, while avoiding also a Gnostic rejection of the material world, gave expression to *creatio ex nihilo* as radical separation or *tzimtzum* (צמצום), meaning "contraction" or "constriction." According to thinkers like Rabbi Nahman of Bratslav (1782-1810), for God to create the world he first had to create nothing. In other words, God had to create first "a vacated space" (חלל פנוי) for creation itself to subsequently fill. This was achieved by God's founding act of contraction, a withdrawing into himself, reducing his essence to an immeasurable point from which there appears a place of possible separation. Within this space God then sends out his rays of emanation (Ayn Sof, אין סוף) — only to be immediately countenanced by his contraction, thereby securing difference again. In this way God is said to be simultaneously transcendent *and* immanent.[17]

---

16. Agata Bielik-Robson, "The Paradox of Radical Transcendence: The Intrigue of Trace in Levinas and Derrida" (seminar paper, Nottingham University, England, June 24, 2005).

17. Arnold Band, *Nahman of Bratslav: The Tales* (New York: Paulist, 1978), p. 285. Similarly, one might also trace the connection with the Christian concept of kenosis (κένωσις), God's self-emptying as the condition of the incarnation, the abasement of the Word (Phil. 2:6).

As Žižek points out — in the context of Schelling — such an account of creation is similar to the modern philosophical procedure introduced by Descartes. In an attempt to ground knowledge, Descartes withdrew into the *cogito* through the exercise of hyperbolic doubt, doubting everything that could be doubted until he arrived at the one thing that could not be doubted: the thinking being. The procedural start is the same.

So whereas in the first instance Schelling's Absolute "wants nothing," it simply "rejoices in its non-being" (ZR, 258), in the second instance the Absolute actively wants this "nothing"; i.e., it wants the nothing as something (AF, 16).[18]

For Žižek, Schelling's account anticipates the Freudian drives. He equates God's act of contraction with his submission to "the chaotic-psychotic universe of blind drives, of their rotary motion, of their undifferentiated pulsating" (ZR, 257) that stands prior to the act of creation proper (i.e., the material world as such). It is these pulsating drives that actively seek the nothing, destroying all determinate content in their path, a state that Žižek puts on a par with a certain "madness" (AF, 8); what Freud called *the death drive*.

In the third instance the beginning proper (i.e., the material beginning) occurs: an act of expansion. What allows for the Absolute to break out from the bind of the drives? As the prologue to Saint John's Gospel suggests: *in the beginning was the Word* (AF, 14); i.e., when one "'finds the word' that breaks the deadlock, the vicious cycle, of empty and confused ruminations" (AF, 15). It is possible to make the connection with psychoanalysis here, in particular Josef Breuer and Freud's momentous discovery that a symptom can be dispelled through the verbal articulation of the cause. For example, in the case of Fräulein Anna O, a young woman suffers *conversion* hysteria; i.e., her psychic conflict was manifest in somatic symptoms including a severe cough, partial paralysis of the right arm, disturbances of vision or hallucinations, and speech disturbances. In the course of their discussions,

---

18. This is Conor Cunningham's definition of nihilism; see Cunningham, *Genealogy of Nihilism* (London: Routledge, 2002), p. xiii. I treat Cunnigham's work in relation to Žižek in more detail in chapter 2 of this work.

Breuer discovered that some of the symptoms disappeared when the young woman was able to provide a detailed account of the memory linked to its original appearance while experiencing the emotions surrounding its appearance. In other words, the symptoms were literally *"talked away"* (SE, 2:35): "Each individual symptom in this complicated case was taken separately in hand; all the occasions on which it had appeared were described in reverse order, starting in time when the patient had become bedridden and going back to the event which had led to its first appearance. When this had been described, the symptom was permanently removed" (SE, 2:35). Returning to Žižek and Schelling, "a Word is pronounced that 'represses,' rejects into the eternal Past, this self-enclosed circuit of drives" (AF, 14). In terms used by Lacan, one can say that by speaking the Word, one substitutes the real of experience for language, and the symbolic, thereby making the transition from the circular motions of the drives to the linear progression of history. Hence, as Žižek points out, on Schelling's reading all material reality is *"proof of the divine madness, of the fact that God himself is out of his mind"* (ZR, 255).

What, then, is the significance of this metamyth for Žižek? "The symbolic order, the universe of the Word, *logos,* can emerge only from the experience of this abyss" (ZR, 253). In other words, all creation, be it at the level of the Absolute or the individual human subject, must make the passage through madness to achieve subjectivity. As Žižek says:

> the ontological necessity of "madness" resides in the fact that it is not possible to pass directly from the "animal soul" immersed in its natural life-world to "normal" subjectivity dwelling in its symbolic universe — the vanishing mediator between the two is the "mad" gesture of radical withdrawal from reality that opens up the space for its symbolic reconstitution. (ZR, 254)

> All reality involves a fundamental antagonism, and is therefore destined to fall prey to Divine fury, to disappear in the "orgasm of forces." Reality is inherently fragile, the result of a balance between contraction and expansion that can, at any moment, explode into one of the extremes. (ZR, 259)

Madness is not therefore simply an aberration of the given order; it is the constitutive moment of becoming human.[19] Žižek clarifies this by pointing to the link between language and subjectivity (i.e., the emergence of the subject in language). In establishing a name for oneself (e.g., John), one "condenses" or "contracts" the wealth of one's being into a mere word; this is simultaneously an act of expansion because the subject "contracts" the core of his being outside himself in an external medium, objectifying himself through a written or spoken sign (ZR, 259). Thereafter the subject is caught within the opposing antagonism that arises when the very medium of being (i.e., language) is the medium of alienation. As Lacan says, "I identify myself in language, but only by losing myself in it as an object" (É, 247/299). To be human, therefore, is not to be identified with the *logos* of reason, as much as madness or alienation.

As Žižek notes, this introduces a radical subversion to the standard Enlightenment subject: "the subject is no longer the Light of Reason opposed to the non-transparent, impenetrable Stuff . . . ; his kernel, the gesture that opens up the space for the Light of Logos, is absolute negativity qua 'night of the world,' the point of utter madness in which fantasmic apparitions of 'partial objects' wander around. Consequently, there is no subjectivity without this gesture of withdrawal" (ZR, 254). Returning to theology, one could say that Christ's cry of dereliction repeats God's own self-abandonment required of creation, which in turn is the dereliction felt by all speaking beings.

The Cry of Dereliction: Desire

According to Žižek, it is God's self-dereliction mirrored in Christ's that constitutes Christianity's unique contribution to Western thought: "Per-

19. In an episode of *The Simpsons* Lisa undertakes an experiment entitled "Is My Brother Dumber Than a Hamster?" A hamster is enticed by booby-trapped food that delivers an electric shock when taken. After receiving a couple of shocks, the hamster quickly learns to avoid the food. Bart is then enticed by a booby-trapped cupcake. Bart receives a shock and tries again, and again, and again, until his synapses are burned out. What makes Bart human is surprisingly the extent to which he pursues pleasure at the cost of his own life — the death drive. Žižek makes this point regarding a rat experiment (OB, 103).

haps the true achievement of Christianity is to elevate a loving (imperfect) Being to the place of God, that is, of ultimate perfection" (PD, 115). For Žižek the Christian God is a God who risks madness in creation and self-dereliction on the cross. In contrast to the Platonic legacy of Greek philosophy, which tended to privilege the eternal realm of ideas at the expense of the material universe — a Gnostic heresy — Christianity privileges precisely these moments of material "imperfection": Christianity makes incompleteness higher than completion (OB, 147). Despite this counterintuitive move, Žižek argues that it is precisely this imperfection that allows for love to emerge: we love the other *because* of the other's imperfection, not despite it (OB, 147). The contrast with Neoplatonism could not be sharper: love is not an integral form in itself, transcendentally securing our love; love emerges from its opposite, the failure of all such attempts.

How, then, does one read that most basic question between young "lovers": *Why do you love me?* It does not do, as Kierkegaard suggests,[20] to write an exacting list of all his or her attributes as if love could be reduced to a series of predicates; to do so would reduce the other to the order of being, of essence, and ultimately of transcendence. If love is marked by anything, it is its ability to disturb the order of being. Love is the very wager upon the emotional uncertainty encountered in another: we love the other *because* the other lacks. Love is therefore of the order of desire. As to the question, it is not asked in such a way as to establish an answer as such, but to establish desire.

The Cry of Dereliction:
The Teleological Suspension of the Ethical

In the theological canon, no one has done more than Søren Kierkegaard to express this paradoxical logic whereby imperfection is higher than perfection. Moreover, Kierkegaard had attended Schelling's lectures in Berlin during the winter of 1841-1842. Žižek makes repeated reference to

20. Kierkegaard, *Philosophical Fragments,* ed. and trans. H. Hong and E. Hong (Princeton: Princeton University Press, 1985), p. 28.

Kierkegaard throughout his works, and so it is helpful to understand something of this formative thinker.[21]

For Kierkegaard the establishment of a religious disposition is preceded by a moment of madness, what he calls the "leap into faith."[22] A leap is required because God is utterly transcendent, *wholly Other*, not something to be immanently recalled from within as if the truth were something to merely discern rather than labor at. Kierkegaard comes to call this act "the teleological suspension of the ethical," whereby one suspends the social and ethical mores, i.e., socially and universally rational claims to what is good in any given situation, a position often associated with Kant's categorical imperative: "I should never act except in such a way *that I can also will that my maxim should become a universal law*";[23] but also reflected in Hegel's *Sittlichkeit*, a collectivist and organic ethical life. In place of the universal, i.e., rational, one must wager on the uncertainty of the Absolute, God, and in doing so admit to one's absolute interest in eternity.[24]

In his most celebrated example, Kierkegaard, writing under the pseudonym Johannes Silentio (John the Silent), grapples with the story of Abraham and the sacrifice of Isaac (the *Akeidah*). Abraham, it will be recalled, had a covenant with God, who had promised he would become the father of a nation. Abraham remained without a son up until his ninety-ninth year, when God again renewed his promise. Soon after, Sarah conceived and gave birth to Isaac; however, the joy was quickly curtailed when Abraham heard again the voice of God, this time commanding him to take Isaac out into the desert and make a sacrifice of him. Yet in the final moment his hand is stayed and God produces a ram to take the place of Isaac.

---

21. DSST, 55; EYS, 70-102; FTKN, 113, 125, 136; FA, 147-48; OSD, 151-56; OB, 45, 77, 105, 148-49; PF, 35, 52, 90, 108-9, 152, 156; PV, 75-80, 86-90, 104-5, 148, 309; RG, 213-15; SOI, 37; TS, 141-42, 211-12, 292-93.

22. S. Kierkegaard, *Concluding Unscientific Postscript*, vol. 1, trans. H. Hong and E. Hong (Princeton: Princeton University Press, 1992), p. 115.

23. Kant, *Grounding for the Metaphysics of Morals*, trans. J. W. Ellington (Indianapolis: Hackett, 1993), p. 14.

24. See S. Kierkegaard, *Repetition/Fear and Trembling*, trans. H. Hong and E. Hong (Princeton: Princeton University Press, 1983), pp. 54-67.

What confounds Silentio is the ethical expression of the story: God commands Abraham to "murder" Isaac.[25] The story seems to contain a moral annulment by making faith *opposed* to ethics, rather than the deepest expression thereof. Yet Abraham is remembered as the father of faith. Silentio reasons therefore that what makes Abraham great is not his moral stature, nor the moral interpretation of his action, but his fidelity to God's word. In other words, what makes Abraham the father of faith is precisely that: *faith.* Abraham remained unflinching in his faith in God against the reason that judged this act murderous.

Kierkegaard was a merciless critic of what we might call the "culturalization of religion," whereby being Christian is primarily an expression of one's cultural heritage or a set of ritual practices rather than an existential, ontological, or, one might add, *political* commitment;[26] and Kierkegaard's meditation on the *Akeidah* was undoubtedly written with the intent to reaffirm Christianity in its scandalous nature, to emphasize its madness in a culture when one was a Christian by virtue of geography rather than belief. In doing so Kierkegaard questioned one of the founding assumptions of Enlightenment rationality: that the ethical is the universal. In other words, the paradox of faith is that the single individual is higher than the universal; i.e., that the right thing to do may at times require eschewing the view that a moral act follows a universally binding form of rationality, be it Kant's categorical imperative or Hegel's *Sittlichkeit,* starting instead with absolute duty to God.[27] For example, in obeying God, Abraham excludes himself thrice: first, from the rational because one believes by virtue of the absurd; second, from the ethical requirement not to kill an innocent human being; and third, from the particular responsibility he owes to his son and family. On all accounts, Abraham occupies the position of an exception.

The anti-Enlightenment thrust of this should not be overlooked. The assumption surrounding the Enlightenment was that peace was best

25. Kierkegaard, *Repetition/Fear and Trembling,* p. 30.

26. Kierkegaard provides the example of the wife of a civil servant who claims she is Christian because she was born in a Christian country. See Kierkegaard, *Concluding Unscientific Postscript,* p. 51.

27. For an overview of the different interpretations, see John Lippitt, *Kierkegaard and Fear and Trembling* (London: Routledge, 2003), pp. 81-109.

served if universal rationality governed in the public arena, while faith was left to personal freedom. Kierkegaard's challenge was to raise the latter above the former.

Silentio calls Abraham "a knight of infinite resignation" — someone who is resigned to give up everything: familiar ties, family duties, love, and ultimately the self; adopting the standpoint of someone absolutely resigned to this loss. The paradox is that Abraham gets to be the father of faith only to the extent that he is prepared to sacrifice his paternity, i.e., kill his beloved son. Hence the moment of infinite resignation is also the movement of faith in which one receives something back (in Abraham's case Isaac). The giving (i.e., the moment of wild abandon in which we are even ready to submit to the death drive) is also the moment of receiving back, a moment of life, and the point one becomes, in Kierkegaard's terms, "a knight of faith." The two moments — giving and receiving — thereby constitute a *double movement,* each occurring at the same time, as found for example in the claim: if you love me, you will let me go.

Given that Kierkegaard had attended Schelling's lectures, it is unsurprising that his account of the double movement of faith chimes with Schelling's account of creation: faith involves a double movement of wild abandonment (contraction), while receiving something back (creation/ expansion): eternity. Faith occupies this position, caught between these two forces: a moment of madness and return.

In attending to Abraham in this way, Kierkegaard makes Abraham the paradigm of Christianity. Christians should be like Abraham, not simply in the sense of *having* faith, but also in the sense of what it means to have faith, i.e., to be exceptional. Christianity is the truly exceptional religion because it is predicated upon the exception, raising it to the level of the whole. Christianity is the paradoxical set of exceptions. In terms of Žižek, one could say that for Kierkegaard, Christianity corresponds to the feminine logic of the *not-All.* Abraham is not an exception to the established rule, the primal father of Freudian mythology who maintains the law while standing outside it; he is one exception among many.

ŽIŽEK

Job and the *Act* of Dereliction

Like Kierkegaard, Žižek does not claim that an act of dereliction or wild abandonment is easy. In his conversations with Glyn Daley and while referring to Schelling, he says "the most horrible thing to encounter for a human being is this abyss of free will" (C, 166), the point where one is not supported by law or social mores (the suspension of the symbolic). He goes on to find an ally in the biblical figure Job. Job's suffering leads his theological interlocutors to argue that "you suffer because you have sinned." However, Job refuses to bow to this theological fatalism (Job 21:7-30). Rather, Job asserts the meaninglessness of his suffering, which Žižek claims opens up a space for a radical ethical act because "the moment you accept suffering as something that does not have a deeper meaning, it means we can change it" (C, 161). This assertion of meaninglessness constitutes in Schelling's terms the moment of madness, the suspension of ethical norms that allows one to reconfigure meaning or act in a way not circumscribed by any given pattern.

As Žižek points out, this is also the basis of Lacanian analysis where the aim is not to restore meaning as such, but the opposite: to show how meaning is always overdetermined, i.e., informed by a plurality of factors; and that it is meaning that subjugates us, not lack of it. By confronting life in its arbitrariness, one suspends the symbolic and is free to act. Said otherwise, the definition of an *act* is a deed whereby one is able to suspend the symbolic supports or networks that sustain subjectivity, opening up an area of "undecidability" in an area that was previously decided.[28] An act is therefore a fundamentally critical gesture, an event that establishes something *new* rather than something subsumed back up into the existing paradigm. In psychoanalytic terms, an act would constitute an action that was not already inscribed by neurotic repetition, such as a person who compulsively hoarded things giving something away.

---

28. Rex Butler, *Slavoj Žižek: Live Theory* (London: Continuum, 2005), p. 68.

Christ's Atonement

Žižek reads Job's suffering as a prefiguration of Christ's suffering. In this way Job provides the key to Žižek's doctrine of atonement. Žižek rejects the four dominant atonement models: First, *the ransom theory:* Christ came "to give his life as a ransom for many" (Mark 10:45). If Christ was the ransom, Žižek argues, "*who demanded this price? To whom* was the ransom paid?" (DSST, 46). Since Christ delivered us from evil, was the ransom paid to Satan? That being the case, "we get the strange spectacle of God and the Devil as partners in exchange." Alternatively, if Christ was offered as a sacrifice to God himself, why precisely did God exact this sacrifice (DSST, 46)? Second, *the psychological reading:* Christ's sacrifice relieves our guilt, proving we are not alone in the world — that God cares for us. But, as Žižek argues, one has to explain this act in *inherent* theological terms, not in terms of psychological mechanisms (DSST, 47). Third, *legalism:* "when there is sin and guilt, there has to be a satisfaction.... However, humanity is not strong enough to provide the satisfaction — only God can do it. The only solution therefore is the incarnation" (DSST, 47). But the problem arises here because *why* should God feel compelled to comply with such a legalistic framework; after all, God is not a thing of the world, he is the creator of it. Why not directly forgive humanity? Fourth: *the edifying-religious moral reason:* if God simply forgave humanity, humanity would not have transformed by itself; Christ's death elicits our compassion and desire to transform ourselves in a free love for God. The problem for Žižek here is that this implies a perverse logic: "is not God strangely akin to the mad governess from Patricia Highsmith's 'Heroine,' who sets the family house on fire in order to be able to prove her devotion to the family by bravely saving the children from the raging flames?" (DSST, 49).

The answer to the atonement lies in Job's claim that suffering is meaningless: Christ's death was meaningless; meaningless for Žižek in the sense that

> Christ's statements ... disturb — or, rather, simply *suspend* — the circular logic of revenge or punishment.... Christ's sacrifice, with its paradoxical structure (it is the very person *against whom* we humans have

37

sinned, whose trust we have betrayed, who atones and pays the prices for our sins), suspends the logic of sin and punishment, of legal or ethical retribution, of "settling accounts," by bringing it to the point of self-relating. The only way to achieve this suspension, break the chain of crime and punishment/retribution, is to assume an utter readiness for self-erasure. And *love,* at its most elementary, is nothing but such a paradoxical gesture of breaking the chain of retribution.... Christ was not sacrificed by and for another, he sacrificed *himself.* (DSST, 49-50)

I quote this passage at some length because it contains the core of Žižek's theology. First: Christ is the self-willed victim who, despite Peter's protestations, freely gives himself over to the chief priests and the scribes to be condemned to death (Mark 10:33). Second, Christ's death performs a psychoanalytic cut, by introducing a moment of madness (the suspension of law or social convention), thereby opening up an area of undecidability. Third, Christ's death is not meant to mediate God in the traditional sense of the word — bridging the abyss of sin between God and humanity so that through the incarnate Christ we have access to the transcendent God — rather, Christ is what Žižek calls the vanishing mediator,[29] whose death (i.e., the death of the big Other) allows God to pass directly into humanity. After the cross "God loses the character of a transcendent Beyond and passes into the Holy Spirit (the spirit of the community of believers).... God is *nothing but* the Holy Spirit of the community of believers. Christ has to die not in order to enable direct communication between God and humanity, but because *there is no longer any transcendent God with whom to communicate*" (DSST, 51).

This is why Žižek calls Christianity the "religion of the cut" (OB, 110) and associates Christianity with trauma (OB, 107). Trauma derives from the Greek: τραῦμα, "to wound"; Christ traumatizes the symbolic networks of supports (i.e., Jewish law) and the systems of retributive justice ("eye for an eye, tooth for a tooth") by committing a senseless act — an act not circumscribed by social convention — a moment of radical negativity. And to this extent Christ can be said to exemplify the death

29. Fredric Jameson, "The Vanishing Mediator; or, Max Weber as Storyteller," in *The Ideologies of Theory: Essays, 1971-1986,* vol. 2 (London: Routledge, 1988), pp. 3-34.

drive: Christ brings into focus the desire for death in his relentless pursuit of Calvary. By manifesting the desire for death, he upsets the sociosymbolic, providing the "cut" that in its very act of destruction (Schelling's contractive force) becomes the moment of — or possibility for — creation (the moment of expansion, i.e., the church).

The Cry of Dereliction: Divine Violence

It is in terms of the cry of dereliction that Žižek identifies "divine violence": just as Christ's cry brings into question the transcendental support of meaning, divine violence is marked by an irruption of the real within the symbolic:

> one should fearlessly identify divine violence with positively existing historical phenomena, thus avoiding all obscurantist mystification. When those outside the structured social field strike "blindly," demanding *and* enacting immediate justice/vengeance, this is "divine violence" — recall, a decade or so ago the panic in Rio de Janeiro when the crowds descended from the *favelas* into the rich part of the city and started looting and burning supermarkets — *this* was "divine violence." . . . Like the biblical locusts, the divine punishment for men's sinful ways, it strikes out of nowhere. . . . It is a decision (to kill, to risk or lose one's own life) made on absolute solitude, not covered by the Big Other.[30]

Divine violence involves a decision and risk. In the above example, these are undertaken by a group of people: those living in the *favelas,* and made in such a way that it involves a suspension of the ethical, i.e., an act not guaranteed by the big Other. Divine violence is therefore an act that of itself remains unsanctioned by the existing framework and as such invokes the passion of risk initially evoked for Žižek by Kierkegaard. It is

---

30. Žižek, "Robespierre, or, the Divine Violence of Terror," in *Žižek Presents Robespierre: Virtue and Terror,* ed. J. Ducange, trans. J. Howe (London and New York: Verso, 2007), pp. x-xi.

"divine" because it represents an intrusion by the *real,* and it is violent because it brings into question the sociosymbolic.

All this raises the very real question: Does Žižek present the theoretical justification for divinely sanctioned acts of terrorism? How, if at all, would he distinguish his own position from the violent expression of religious fundamentalism? First, one can return to Kierkegaard's original discussions. For Kierkegaard, a suspension of the ethical is not an *abandonment* of the ethical, not least because it already assumes the ethical, i.e., that God *is* Goodness himself — just as the religious emphasis on the particular reworks the aesthetic emphasis on individuality. Second, one could return to the *Akeidah* and read it more generally in terms of the tragic awareness that some choices prevail *as* impossible extremes, and yet one must still act. So, it is not the case that in a given situation, such as obeying God or sacrificing your child, one should always obey God. After all, who is to decide whether God's call is legitimate or not? How would one differentiate between psychotics such as Peter Sutcliffe (the Yorkshire Ripper) who claim to have been obeying the voice of God, and the authentic voice of God?

It is in the sense of the "tragic awareness of the act" that Žižek reads Kierkegaard. Hence he describes divine violence as "extra-moral"[31] — not in the sense of immoral (senseless killing) but in the sense of a purposeful act that intervenes in such a way as to allow the contradiction between violence and justice to coincide just as God's justice can be said to coincide with the terror of the plagues. Žižek's point is not that God sent divine plagues as punishment, and so in extreme cases one can justify a bit of violence; but that a spontaneous act of violence, arbitrary in nature like a plague or famine, can coincide with a sense of justice or critique. For example, extreme weather patterns provide a judgment upon our ecological management of the planet. To avoid any confusion on this point, Žižek says: one must "fearlessly identify divine violence with positively existing historical phenomena" to avoid any mystification of violence. This avoids the charge that he gives license to terrorist acts in the name of God. Rather, it is an exegetical practice, a practice of reading those areas historically in terms of God's condemnation, to allow a criti-

---

31. Žižek, "Robespierre," p. xi.

cal judgment to occur through the suffering contradiction whereby violence on the part of the oppressed coincides with justice.

The Theological Critique of Violence

It is at this point that I want to critically engage Žižek's theology, both as
theology and as it relates to his project to reactualize the Left as a radical
political force. My contention concerns the following. On the one hand,
Žižek's support of Christianity is predicated upon its transgressive nature; i.e., it breaks with the ethical or the symbolic, a retributive justice
associated with sacrificial economies of atonement. Yet on the other
hand his entire theoretical apparatus is predicated upon such a sacrificial system. In other words, his fundamental ontology undercuts any appeal to Christianity as the exemplar of revolutionary logic on the
grounds of a preferred violence. Simply put, Žižek remains locked into
the very retributive system he is critical of. To take a simple example: to
justify divine violence by appeal to the Old Testament God of wrath is to
remain within the very viewpoint his theology is critical of: a retributive
God. This is not simply a matter of inconsistency, but of whether a really
critical revolution by the Left can be built upon the presumption of violence. To establish my argument, and develop it, I refer to the work of
René Girard.

Girard

Few anthropologists/theologians have done as much to clarify the distinction between a sacrificial economy of violence and one of peaceable
difference as René Girard. Indeed, Žižek not only credits Girard with providing the paradigmatic account of sacrificial logic (EYS, 73), but he also
directly attributes his own reading of Job to Girard: "We can follow René
Girard — it was precisely for this reason that we encounter in the Jewish
religion the first appearance of a subject who *resists* assuming the role of
a scapegoat/victim: Job. Job's refusal to play his part in the sacrificial rite
is the exact reverse of his perplexion in front of the calamities: instead of

identifying heroically with his evil fate, he continues to raise the question of the meaning of it all" (EYS, 56). Born in Avignon in 1923, Girard has spent most of his life in America, where he has taught and undertaken research across a range of disciplines including literary paleontology, criticism, historiography, comparative religion, anthropology, and psychology. He was central in promoting critical theory in America during the sixties, organizing conferences with Derrida, Lacan, and the like, but it was his work concerning Christianity, sacrifice, and violence that brought him to international acclaim. He made the argument for a universal anthropological theory of violence and sacrifice to which the Gospels offered an exceptional alternative (Girard had a dramatic conversion at the age of thirty-six). Beginning with violence and aggression, Girard argued that these could be traced back to the mimetic character of desire: we desire objects not for their intrinsic value as such, but because they are themselves desired by others. Desire operates within a threefold structure: the subject, the object of desire, and an entity that mediates desire (or as Lacan puts it, "man's desire is the desire of the other"). Conflict subsequently arises out of the inevitable rivalry that competition for the object generates. It is in contrast to the usual assumption that *difference* breeds conflict that Girard argues that the cause of rivalry is "sameness and similarity."[32]

Murderous violence is averted only through a scapegoat mechanism. A sacrificial victim must be found, a nodal point around which the group can coalesce, to focus their collective envy. The death of the scapegoat placates the aggression and provides a channel of release that reestablishes the social bond. And, as Žižek explains, "as if in recognition of this beneficial role he plays, the victim thus gains the aura of sanctity" (EYS, 73). In this way the scapegoat is said to suffer a *double transference,* loathed in the act of expulsion, only to be subsequently exalted.

The mechanism of the scapegoat is characteristically obscured because the scapegoat is a substitute victim, not chosen for any intrinsic quality as such, but simply as a substitute. This redoubling or surrogacy not only obscures the murderous quality of all human desire, it forms the

32. René Girard, *Violence and the Sacred,* trans. P. Gregory (London and New York: Continuum, 2005), p. 155.

basis of all ritual action: to sacrifice or scapegoat is to practice the model form of religion.

Returning to desire, its mimetic nature creates a *double bind* upon the subject, a contradictory double imperative because "man cannot respond to that universal human injunction 'Imitate me!' without almost immediately encountering an inexplicable counter order 'Don't imitate me!' (which really means, 'Do not appropriate without almost immediately encountering an inexplicable counter order "Don't imitate me!"' (which really means, 'Do not appropriate *my* object')."[33]

The double bind accounts for the self-perpetuating nature of the process. Where someone desires, and encounters the obstacle of conflicting desires, the very rebuffs strengthen the resolve of desire. So by a "mental shortcut"[34] violence is seen as a distinctive attribute of the goal, and thus violence and desire become inevitably linked. Violence thereby becomes "the signifier of ultimate desire, of divine self-sufficiency, of that 'beautiful totality' whose beauty depends on its being inaccessible and impenetrable."[35]

Lacan on Sacrifice

For psychoanalysis to provide a successful critique of social relations (i.e., to truly become a social psychology), one has to be able to show how the structure of society corresponds to the structure of the psyche. Lacan and Žižek do this ably by showing the relation between the Oedipal law and language. Similarly, to make Girard's argument really pertinent to the criticism of Žižek, one has to be able to show the relation between Girard's account of the founding murder and Žižek's account of subjectivity, because it cannot be simply a matter of opposing Girard to Žižek, but of showing how Girard anticipates and clarifies much of Žižek's work, while developing it in ways that respond to the perceived difficulties in Žižek's work.

33. Girard, *Violence and the Sacred*, p. 156.
34. Girard, *Violence and the Sacred*, p. 157.
35. Girard, *Violence and the Sacred*, p. 157.

In *Enjoy Your Symptom* Žižek establishes the link between Girard's thesis and Lacan: both advance a theory that refuses sacrificial logic. For Lacan, "the sacrifice signifies that, in the object of our desires, we try to find evidence for the presence of the desire of this Other that I call here *the dark God*" (SXI, 275). Or, as Žižek says: "In its most fundamental dimension sacrifice is a 'gift of reconciliation' to the Other, destined to appease its desire. Sacrifice conceals the abyss of the Other's desire, more precisely: it conceals the Other's lack, inconsistency. . . . *Sacrifice is a guarantee that 'the Other exists':* that there *is* an Other who can be appeased by means of the sacrifice" (EYS, 56). Sacrifice is not concerned with offering up an object desired by another; rather, it functions to give body to the Other. Sacrifice involves an object at the level of the imaginary phallus, an object meant to domesticate the trauma of the real that threatens to break in at any moment. Sacrifice follows the logic of castration: *pars pro toto:* the part for the whole: an object is ceded in the hope of securing the imaginary whole.[36] This logic is exemplified in the book of Exodus, when Yahweh is about to kill Moses but is dissuaded from his abrupt circumcision by his wife (Exod. 4:24-26). His sacrifice ensures that he gives presence to the terrifying God. One could say therefore that sacrifice accords to the logic of metaphysics, whereby a part sacrificed sustains a sense of imaginary wholeness. Lacan's resistance to the logic of sacrifice is therefore the attempt to move beyond metaphysics, to challenge the very idea that a big Other exists. And, by resisting the retributive logic of sacrifice, the implication is that one identifies with the *lack* in the Other.

However, by extending the comparison of Girard's theory to Lacan's work as a whole, it is possible to show how Lacan and Žižek remain secretly wedded to the logic of sacrifice, which leads to an impasse in their work.

To begin with, consider Lacan's early work on the mirror stage and fragmented body. As Richard Johnson has argued,

In the life of a civilisation the fragmentary body corresponds to the initial lack of social differentiation which brings on the mimetic crisis,

---

36. H. Zwart, "Medicine, Symbolisation and the 'Real' Body," *Journal of Medicine, Healthcare, and Philosophy* 1 (May 1998): 107-17.

the stage that precedes the formation of any "social contract" or symbolic order. The mirror image is the monstrous double, the surrogate victim who promises to bring wholeness by standing in for the community as a whole. It is thus synonymous with the phallus, which is nothing but the imaginary "I" whose sacrifice gives birth to the ego ideal. Through the murder of the monstrous double the war of all against all is transformed into the unanimous violence of all against one which establishes the differential system of the social order. This is the origin of monarchy and government (the big Other), the minus one or exception which grounds the law (also the cult of celebrity etc). The function of the symbolic rituals and prohibitions is to maintain the differences which prevent society from descending into mimetic rivalry and reciprocal violence. Alienation sets in when the impact of the founding murder has receded into oblivion and even its ritual re-enactments have fallen into disuse, heralding the advent of another mimetic crisis.[37]

Similarly, consider Žižek's claim that "between the primordial Real of the pure Multiple and the symbolic universe there is a vanishing mediator, the gesture of/in the Real that grounds symbolization itself, the violent opening up of a gap in the Real which is not yet symbolic" (TS, 239 n. 2). The Real corresponds to the sacred, the uncontrollable violence that can be averted only by the sacrifice or expulsion of the imaginary thing, what Žižek calls the "vanishing mediator." The sacrifice establishes the operations of the signifier, the instillation of the symbolic function. And this is why for Žižek there can be no symbolic action that has not been paid for by "murder" (ZR, vii). As Richard Boothby says, sacrifice, like language, is situated on the pivot between the imaginary and the symbolic, exemplified in the act of reading the entrails of a sacrifice animal — staging the transition from nature to nature. Sacrifice, like castration, is "the gateway through which the subject comes to language."[38]

In summary, then, while Lacan and Žižek advocate a move beyond

---

37. Richard Johnson, e-mail message to author, March 3, 2006.

38. Richard Boothby, *Freud as Philosopher* (London and New York: Routledge, 2001), p. 183.

the sacrificial logic of metaphysics, they nonetheless hold on fast to it by weaving it into normative accounts of symbolic interaction: speech comes about through violence and death; violence and death become the horizon of speech. Arguably this is what leads Žižek to defend divine violence rather than make the metacritical shift and resist violence in toto.

Girard's Critique

It would be easy to read the Gospels according to a similar logic: Christ is the scapegoat, the innocent victim who must pay the price of sin, i.e., be cast out to ensure human solidarity. Moreover, like the scapegoat, Christ experiences the double transference of the crowd: initially vilified, he is then heralded as a savior for resolving the mimetic crisis. However, what is really radical about Girard is that he rejects the whole edifice of sacrifice, including its psychoanalytic variation, on the basis of the Hebrew Scriptures and the Gospels. Psychoanalysis enshrines foundational violence in the Oedipus complex. Oedipus is the scapegoat who unwittingly kills his father and marries his mother; cast out of Thebes to secure social cohesion, he is vilified in *Oedipus Rex,* only to be transfigured by the gods in *Oedipus at Colonus,* thereby taking on the double transference of the crowd. Yet according to Girard, the Bible texts, and especially the New Testament, do away with sacrifice by exposing the founding mechanism of society, i.e., the way societies are formed in opposition to an arbitrary victim or scapegoat. Rather than viewing Christ's death as satisfying God's desire for a sacrificial lamb, Girard identifies "the real meaning and function of the Passion" as "one of subverting sacrifice and barring it from working ever again by forcing the founding mechanism out into the open, writing it down in the text of all the Gospels."[39] Christ's sacrifice was not part of some bizarre pact Christ secretly made with God that called for his murder to satisfy God's wrath. Christ has no place in support of a violent revolution; Christ met violence and suffering without re-

---

39. René Girard, *Things Hidden since the Foundation of the World,* trans. Stephen Bann and Michael Metteer (Stanford: Stanford University Press, 1987), p. 181.

taliation, but with forgiveness; *God is defeated by violence on the cross, because violence has no place in God's kingdom.* By refusing violence, Christ's sacrifice brings into question the very nature of sacrifice, constituting, as it were, the very sacrifice *of* sacrifice. As Girard explains, "The Christ of the Gospels dies against sacrifice, and through his death, he reveals its nature and origin by making sacrifice unworkable, at least in the long run, and bringing sacrificial culture to an end."[40] There is, Girard argues, nothing in the Gospels to suggest that Christ's death was a sacrifice in the traditional sense of the word; to say Christ's death was sacrifice makes sense only when what is sacrificed is sacrifice itself.

The opposition between violence and nonviolence is repeated in the distinction between myth and gospel. Myth refers principally to a story that occludes the mechanism of violence through the scapegoat; gospel exposes the violence of the mechanism.

Again, the Girardian overtones of Žižek's work in this regard are explicit. For example, consider his paraphrasing of Badiou's event in *The Fragile Absolute:* "The Event is the impossible Real of a structure, of its synchronous symbolic order, the engendering violent gesture which brings about the legal Order that renders this very gesture retroactively 'illegal,' relegating it to the spectral repressed status of something that can never be fully acknowledged-symbolised-confessed. In short, the synchronous structural Order is a kind of defence-formation against its grounding Event which can be discerned only in the guise of a mythical spectral narrative" (FA, 92). The structural order or legality is engendered by an act of violence, a founding sacrifice in which a victim (identified with the event) is ejected as condition of social cohesion. Žižek identifies this process not simply as giving rise to *myth;* but that myth is constituted by a narrative occlusion of the real, Girard's point exactly, that it is myth, as opposed to gospel, which occludes the victimage mechanism by imputing some misdemeanor to an innocent scapegoat.

It is in the light of Girard that we should return to Žižek's definition of divine violence. It is not that Žižek's account of divine violence requires some refinement, but that the very link established between divinity and violence should be refused. This is Girard's position: *to refuse*

40. James Williams, ed., *The Girard Reader* (New York: Herder Crossroads, 2001), p. 18.

the very category of divine violence, because violence cannot be divine in origin.[41] What makes Žižek think that an event can be interpreted as the Old Testament wrath of God is that these images and texts describe the mimctic and sacrificial crisis often brought about in times of famine, as with the descent from the *favelas.* However, it is precisely the economy of sacrifice that is subverted in the Hebrew Bible and the Gospels. A case in point is the *Akeidah.* In taking the Kierkegaardian line Žižek arguably misses the crucial historicist point: God's staying of Abraham's hand, and the substitution of a nonhuman for a human, already points one in the direction of a nonviolent form of revolution, the displacement of human sacrifice with animal sacrifice, a dramatic shift in the evolution of culture. Žižek's omission of this point is all the more surprising as he explicitly bases his reading of Job as one who resists the role of scapegoat on the basis of Girard's lead (EYS, 56). By failing to attend to this, Žižek's theoretical endeavor arguably becomes complicit in perpetuating the very mechanism he criticizes.[42]

Dereliction

One can further this contention by paying heed to Žižek's persistent misquoting of Christ's cry of dereliction.[43] He replaces the more impersonal "God [Ελωι]" of Mark and Matthew with the more personal "Father [Πατήρ]," so instead of reading it as "God, why hast thou forsaken me?"

41. Girard, *Things Hidden,* pp. 85-190.

42. Milbank has argued that Girard is guilty of an anthropological quasi-scientific reduction of religion to a single phenomenon: sacrifice. Moreover, he suggests that there is little evidence that our cities and towns arose through a riotous act. Milbank, *Theology and Social Theory,* 2nd ed. (Oxford: Blackwell, 2006), pp. 395-402. However, as J. Bottum points out, "We need only notice that every culture manifests in its myths a deep terror of the breakdown of all distinctions and the mimetic escalation of violence. Against this threatened violence of all against all, cultural myth poses the solution of another violence: the violence of all against one." J. Bottum, "Girard among the Girardians," *First Things* 61 (1996): 42-45; http://www.leaderu.com/ftissues/ft9603/articles/revessay.html (accessed August 16, 2007).

43. See, for example, PD, 171; OB, 145; PV, 106. This question was first posed to me by Conor Cunningham.

he takes it to read "Father, why hast thou forsaken me?" (PD, 171; OB, 145; PV, 106). In doing so, he conflates two pivotally distinct yet related events: Christ's forsakenness by God (Ελωι) in Matthew and his committal back to the Father (Πατήρ) in Luke. Yet, as Milbank points out:

> Christ was never merely abandoned, even for a single instance. Even though all his friends deserted him in the garden of Gethsemane and he suffered thereby the worst extremity of human agony, he still did not endure ontological desertion. The cry of dereliction upon the cross recorded by Matthew and Mark (Matthew 27:46; Mark 15:34) involves no abandonment by the Father, but rather Jesus' deepest entering into the self-separation of sinful humanity from God: hence it is to God [Ελωι], not the Father [Πατήρ] ("My God, my God . . .") that Jesus as Son in his humanity cries out. When, by contrast, Jesus in his divine nature speaks as the Son to the Father [Πατήρ], it is a question of serene deliverance in contrast to the cruel human handing over: "Father, into thy hands I commit my Spirit!" (Luke 23:46).[44]

Utter abandonment also shapes Žižek's reading of Kierkegaard. He takes Kierkegaard's teleological suspension of the ethical to imply a moment of utter abandonment, where abandonment means a break from all existing norms. Yet this is clearly at odds with Kierkegaard, for whom the teleological suspension of the ethical implies the obverse: it is not abandonment *from* but abandonment *to* God. This is part of the double movement of faith by which in giving everything up one receives infinitely more back, or said otherwise, one receives back infinity.

By misquoting the passage Žižek is able to give the last word to abandonment, and this has profound moral and political consequences for his work as a whole. Chiefly, because it confirms the subject as subject qua victim, i.e., *the one abandoned*, which undermines the possibility or potential for political action, the very obverse of Žižek's stated aim.

This criticism can be further developed with reference to Žižek's "speculative" standpoint, an approach that owes something to the intellectual mystic Gillian Rose, whose restatement of Hegel is credited by

---

44. Milbank, *Being Reconciled: Ontology and Pardon* (London: Routledge, 2003), p. 98.

Žižek in *For They Know Not What They Do* (FTKN, 103). In *Hegel contra Sociology*, published in 1981, Rose set out to reactualize Marxist social theory by returning to Hegelian "speculative experience." Rose contested the popular reading of Hegel according to which Hegel's *Phenomenology* presented a grandiose account of an evolving and unfolding consciousness that was able to *sublate* (i.e., absorb) its objects into itself, overcoming "the duality of the knower and known, so that consciousness is left without an outside."[45] Such an all-absorbing attitude was taken by many of the so-called post-structuralists (e.g., Derrida and Lacan) to be incapable of construing difference in its integrity because difference is always absorbed back into the system. This was the basis of Lacan's critique of Hegel in "The Subversion of the Subject and the Dialectic of Desire." Here he explicitly situates Hegel's *Phenomenology* along the imaginary axis; i.e., it is ruled by sameness (É, 675/798).

Yet in *Hegel contra Sociology* a different picture of Hegel emerges, one in which error takes on a philosophical importance. According to Rose, Hegel's *Phenomenology* invites the reader to enter a process that highlights the way thought or natural consciousness *undermines* itself, but not toward some grand theoretical reconciliation (the criticism of Hegel), nor the apparent postmodern alternative: despairing skepticism and melancholia.

Herein lies the significance of Hegel's "speculative proposition." As Rose explains, in its ordinary form a proposition is usually divided into the subject and its predicate, joined by the copula "is" (e.g., the cat is black). The subject is considered the fixed bearer of variable accidents (i.e., the grammatical predicates), with the proposition affirming an identity between the two (e.g., cat and black). However,

> Hegel knew that his thought would be misunderstood if it were read
> as a series of ordinary propositions, which affirm an identity between
> a fixed subject and contingent accidents, but he also knew that, like
> any thinker, he had to present his thought in propositional form. He
> thus proposed, in an unfortunately schematic statement, that the

45. Rowan Williams, "Between Politics and Metaphysics: Reflection in the Wake of Gillian Rose," *Modern Theology* 11, no. 1 (1995): 3-22, 9.

propositional form must be read as a "speculative proposition." This use of "speculative" is not the same as Kant's use of it. It does not refer to the illegitimate use of correct principles. . . . To read a proposition "speculatively" means that the identity which is affirmed between subject and predicate is seen equally to affirm a lack of identity between subject and predicate. This reading implies an identity different from a merely formal one of the ordinary proposition. This different kind of identity cannot be pre-judged, that is, it cannot be justified in a transcendental sense, and it cannot be stated in a proposition of the kind to be eschewed. This different kind of identity must be understood as a result to be achieved. From this perspective the subject is not fixed, nor the predicate accidental: they acquire their meaning in a series of relations to each other. Only when the lack of identity between the subject and predicate has been experienced, can their identity be grasped.[46]

How does this anticipate Žižek's Marxism? The crucial point for Žižek is that it is the very lack of identity in the speculative relation that encourages the work of actuality, i.e., social negotiation. Because if thinking follows this pattern of self-displacement, then it becomes problematic to speak of a reality in which we exist as atomized individuals whose goals can be specified in mutual isolation; as it does also to speak of subjects who are "bearers of economic functions, such as 'capitalist' and 'worker.'"[47] Nor can it become a question of delivering a social utopian ideal. Instead, it becomes a matter of showing how the model of consciousness, as a property-owning individual who accumulates objects, is an incoherent myth, a misrepresentation of the workings of natural consciousness; and finally by linking this to the analysis of the economy, it creates the conditions for a revolutionary practice. Yet it is questionable whether Žižek's work is able to carry through this projected goal.

In his defense, it may be argued first that despite the emphasis on abandonment, one is not abandoned *as such;* on the contrary, it is the very feeling of abandonment that negatively constitutes our relation to

---

46. Gillian Rose, *Hegel contra Sociology* (London: Athlone, 1981), pp. 48-49.
47. Rose, *Hegel contra Sociology,* p. 216.

the other. Said otherwise, I understand the other at the point I recognize that the other doesn't understand himself or herself. Žižek accounts for the God-relation in this way in what amounts to a Lacanian atheology: it is the *lack of identity that informs the God relation,* or as Žižek says, "only when I experience the infinite pain of separation from God do I share an experience with God Himself" (PD, 91). That is to say, "our radical experience of the separation from God is the very feature which unites us with him" (PD, 91; PV, 106): *Abyssus abyssum invocat.*[48]

In a review of Gillian Rose's work, Rowan Williams restages Hegel's question: How do "we come to think of thinking in the framework of dispossession"?[49] The answer: it requires a history that can be told as the narrative of the absolute's self-loss and recovery. In other words, "certain models of thinking come to be available because of the presence of certain narratives about God and God's people, narratives that insist on speaking of divine displacement in one sense or another"[50] — for example, a God who articulates his action through that which is other to the divine, or a God who dies on the cross and resurrects; moreover, this becomes the model of the apostle who abrogates the self in order to represent the noninterest of God, but who in turn must be disposed of that very identity: Israel's identity becomes bound up with exile; Jesus' identity with the cross; while the church becomes bound up with the imagery of the "resident alien."[51]

Williams's account includes something missing in Žižek's: resurrection; without it abandonment has the final say. When this happens, one can identify with the other only in terms of abandonment, i.e., with a victim as victim. This identification not only confirms victimhood, thereby diminishing us all, but it also undermines the very potential for political action that it seeks to establish.

---

48. Aquinas makes a not dissimilar claim: "we are joined to him as to something unknown"; *Summa Theologiæ* 1a, q. 12 a. 13 ad 1.

49. Williams "Between Politics and Metaphysics," p. 18.

50. Williams "Between Politics and Metaphysics," p. 20.

51. Williams "Between Politics and Metaphysics," p. 19.

CHAPTER 2

Belief before Belief

Robert Pfaller has pointed out that the theorist of ideology, like the psychoanalyst, does not need to know "how things really are" to recognize a given idea as ideological; the theorist of ideology need only recognize that "this idea represents an object differently from the one it explicitly speaks about."[1] For Marx the ideological system par excellence was religious, keeping the mass of humanity in slavery and bondage by promising an afterlife, while all the time maintaining the existing domination. And because religion had its place in the foundation of culture, "the criticism of religion is the prerequisite of all critique."[2] For Marx this had been almost completed in Germany by Ludwig Feuerbach: man makes religion; religion does not make man. Now, only the practical task remained. In Žižek's work, by contrast, religion is the prerequisite of the critique of ideology. The religious critique of metaphysics is the first critique of ideology, and therefore the critique of ideology already assumes the religious standpoint. In the first part of this chapter I explore Žižek's controversial claim, and how it arises from both developments within Marxism and his appropriation of the book of Job, and his theology of dereliction.

In the second part I take seriously Matthew Sharpe's skepticism re-

---

1. Robert Pfaller, "Where Is Your Hamster? The Concept of Ideology in Žižek's Cultural Theory," in *Traversing the Fantasy: Critical Responses to Slavoj Žižek*, ed. G. Boucher, J. Glynos, and M. Sharpe (Aldershot: Ashgate, 2005), pp. 105-24, 108.

2. Karl Marx, "Towards a Critique of Hegel's *Philosophy of Right:* Introduction," in *Karl Marx: Selected Writings*, ed. D. McLellan (Oxford: Oxford University Press, 1977), p. 63.

garding Žižek's project. Is he able to sustain an ideological critique? In many ways Sharpe's criticisms anticipate my own: that a radical vision requires more than the ontological impossibilism that Lacan leaves us with; it requires a more positive account of creation. However, where Sharpe ends, my argument begins: the problem with Žižek's critique of ideology is not that it is rooted in theology, but that it is not theological enough. Drawing on the work of Conor Cunningham, I highlight the nihilism that underpins Žižek's ontology. But rather than simply oppose nihilism to theology, I show the overlap between Cunningham's theological critique of nihilism and Žižek's critique of onto-theology. By giving a more theologically grounded critique of ideology to Žižek, I suggest a more optimistic reading that is thereby able to respond to the concerns of Žižek's critics. I begin by explaining something of Marx's theory of ideology.

Reality Is Ideological

What is the status of ideology today? Marx's theory of ideology tended to uncritically assume the dichotomy of reality and fantasy: reality was a pure space of the given to be objectively discerned once the cobwebs of superstition — be it religion or class — were wiped away. It was as if there were a series of competing narratives versus some extradiscursive reality, and the true narrative (exploitation of the working classes) was the one that best fitted the facts. In short, ideology works at the level of knowledge: what matters is that our language about the world corresponds to the world as real.

However, as Lacan points out, the very distinction between true and false takes place only *within* language (É, 436/524). It cannot be the case, therefore, that language simply reflects the world as real; rather, it creates it as real. So, to take the ideological critique of religion as an example, the standard criticism centers on whether God actually exists, i.e., whether God's existence is objectively true on the basis of empirical grounds. And because belief in God cannot be empirically verified, religion is seen to be obscuring reality. By contrast, taking Lacan into account, the emphasis now falls upon the way the subject represents God, i.e., how the concept of God works discursively. Or, as Robert Pfaller says, what matter are the "conditions for the production of the idea, not its apparent truth-value with regard to empirical data."[3]

The shift from reality as given to reality as constructed can already be traced through Freud's work in his rejection of the "seduction theory." Faced with children's accounts of seduction, Freud initially assumed these were actual accounts of sexual advances by adults, and it was this traumatic experience that served as the basis for sexual repression (SE, 1:238-39). However, given the sheer volume of reports, Freud was led to abandon this model, recognizing instead that many accounts were already the product of a phantasmal creation, the disguised expression of a wish fulfillment (SE, 7:274). In short, Freud shifted his understanding of sexual repression from the question of objectivity (it really happened) to subjectivity (the way the child constructs reality).

This shift in perspective was the basis of Althusser's critique of Marx, for which he famously drew upon Lacan.[4] According to Althusser, ideology is not simply a lie, but refers to the way one is "interpellated" into existing symbolic structures such as family, church institutions, and rituals — what Althusser called "Ideological State Apparatus" — in such a way as to maintain and reproduce individuals who willingly participate in the existing process of production. Ideology is not an extradiscursive layer, but is embodied in the material practices that constitute life. Returning to the example of religion, it can be said that belief is less an internal dispossession of the will than a material practice. In other words, belief is exterior. This is exactly Žižek's point: "Religious belief . . . is not merely, or even primarily, an inner conviction; but the Church as an institution and its rituals (prayers, baptism, confirmation, confession . . .) which far from being a mere secondary externalisation of the inner belief, stands for the very mechanism that generates it" (ZR, 65-66).

But how precisely does this work? Here Žižek refers to the Freudian concept of *Nachträglichkeit* (deferred action). In Freud's view of psychic causality, a memory trace or experience could be retroactively reconfigured in the light of a new experience. To take language as an example,

3. Pfaller, "Where Is Your Hamster?" p. 106.

4. Louis Althusser, "Freud and Lacan," in Althusser, *Lenin and Philosophy, and Other Essays* (New York and London: Monthly Review Press, 1971), pp. 189-220.

the final word of a sentence or paragraph has the power to retroactively change the meaning of all that went before (e.g., I was batting my . . . eyelid/heart out/etc.).[5] Likewise the problem of ideology resides at the level where the narratives themselves retroactively determine what we experience *as* reality. For this reason Žižek says "reality is already ideological" and *"Ideological is not the 'false-consciousness' of a (social) [or transcendental] being but this being itself in so far as it is supported by 'false-consciousness'"* (SOI, 21).

Žižek extends Althusser's work in the direction of Lacan's concept of fantasy. Within the context of psychoanalysis, fantasy is a kind of screen, providing a protective layer between primary repression and secondary overlay, thereby separating drives (the real) from desire (symbolic), and hence organizing desire. For example, in *Silence of the Lambs,* Hannibal Lector skillfully reconstructs Agent Starling's childhood desire to save a lamb from slaughter on her father's farm as the motivating factor in her work as a police officer: her desire to save the politician's child is really the desire to save the lamb and hence herself from symbolic castration — because animal sacrifice classically stages the transition from nature to culture. In this way her initial fantasy organizes her desire, and hence fantasy is not a category opposed *to* reality; rather, it is psychically constructive *of* reality.

Fantasy provides an answer to the question posed by the other: *Che vuoi?* (what do you want?). In the encounter with another we are confounded by the surplus of meaning that exceeds language, mopping it up into our interpretive framework rather than accepting it in its sheer arbitrariness. For example, the question "Why don't you go out and get the newspaper?" can be heard quite literally: the desire for a newspaper, or as a demand to be rid of the other: "Are you trying to get rid of me?" Fantasy covers up the inconsistencies within the symbolic order, and hence at its most basic, one can say *ideology is that which tries to obfuscate the real.*

In the course of analysis the analyst must reconstruct the analysand's

5. This is also the basis of the Christian concept of typographical readings of the Old Testament. See Henri de Lubac, "Spiritual Understanding," trans. Luke O'Neill, in *The Theological Interpretation of Scripture: Classic and Contemporary Readings,* ed. Stephen Fowl (Oxford: Blackwell, 1997), pp. 3-25, 6.

fundamental fantasy, so as to understand the way the analysand organizes desire. The aim is then to open the subject up to the lack that accompanies the symbolic (i.e., all our interpretive communication), a process Lacan calls *traversing the fantasy.*

Traversing the Fantasy

As Richard Boothby says, when Lacan describes the aim of analysis as traversing the fantasy, he does not mean one abandons fantasy for reality, but the opposite: one submits to the effect of symbolic lack.[6] In *The Puppet and the Dwarf* Žižek proposes the book of Job as the "first exemplary case of the critique of ideology in human history" (PD, 125). In other words, Job *traverses the fantasy.* The story of Job is well known: God allows Satan to put to the test his most virtuous devotee. Satan then systematically destroys Job's riches, property, livestock, servants, and children, the events of which provide for a sustained argument between Job and his theological interlocutors on the nature of suffering. Žižek reads Job as follows:

> Contrary to the usual notion of Job, he is *not* a patient sufferer, enduring his ordeal with a firm faith in God — on the contrary, he complains all the time, rejecting his fate. . . . When the three theologians-friends visit him, their line of argumentation is the standard ideological sophistry (if you are suffering, you must by definition have done something wrong, since God is just). . . . Job's proper ethical dignity lies in the way he persistently rejects the notion that his suffering can have any meaning, either [as] punishment for his past sins or the trial of his faith. (PD, 125)

How does this constitute *traversing the fantasy?* To accept the meaningfulness of Job's suffering would involve making the metaphysical gesture — i.e., positing some cause (sin) or system (retributive jus-

---

6. Richard Boothby, *Freud as Philosopher* (London and New York: Routledge, 2001), p. 275.

tice) that secures the meaningfulness of events in terms of justice. But Job's response is *antimetaphysical* in the sense that it refuses any fantasmic screen through which events are organized. Job simply accepts the meaninglessness of suffering. However, and herein lies the sting for Žižek, it is when we learn the meaninglessness of suffering that we cease to be tyrannized by it.

Žižek underlines this point with reference to the address God makes to Job toward the end of the book. In a somewhat "tempestuous spirit" (Job 38:1) God says:

> Brace yourself like a fighter;
> now it is my turn to ask questions and yours to inform me.
> Where were you when I laid the earth's foundations?
> Tell me, since you are so well informed!
> Who decided the dimensions of it, do you know?
> Or who stretched the measuring line across it?
> What supports its pillars at its base?
>
> (Job 38:3-6)

Žižek calls this an example of "rhetorical boasting" (PD, 126), the supreme display of God's power that, not unlike the bully, masks a certain impotence. Indeed, Žižek's God appears to occupy the subject position of the hysteric, the subject who keeps asking questions to avoid the possibility of actually having to listen to the answer. In his response Job maintains his silence, which opens up the interpretive space. "In a gesture of silent solidarity, he perceived the divine impotence. God is neither just nor unjust, simply impotent. What Job suddenly understood was that it *was not him, but God Himself, who was actually on trial in Job's calamities,* and He failed the test miserably" (PD, 126-27). It is not then the case, as it was for some patristic writers, that, faced with the inexplicable question of suffering, one had not to reason but rather to trust in God's all-encompassing power. Rather, one has to transpose the difficulty that humanity faces in the light of these questions into God himself. It is not that God secretly knows the answer to why existence is marked by suffering and hence we should trust his motivations, however hidden; it is that there is no secret and hence no answer.

For this reason Žižek insists on the parallel between Job and Christ: "Job foresaw God's own future suffering" (PD, 127). Job's assertion that suffering is meaningless corresponds to Christ's because Christ's suffering was also meaningless; meaningless in the sense that it cannot be sensibly reduced to a sacrifice in an economy of exchange; rather, Christ freely gives himself, an act of wild abandonment that suspends the circular logic of crime and retribution. As Milbank puts it, if Christ's death constitutes a sacrifice in any sense of the word, it is as a sacrifice of the very concept of sacrifice.

In sum, the critique of ideology is the critique of onto-theology, the overcoming of metaphysics. The critique of ideology involves suspending the transcendental scheme that configures reality, bringing the entire sociosymbolic into question, and submitting oneself entirely to the effects of the signifier.

This same point can be made with reference to the big Other — the Other that is irreducible to any really existing other — the onto-theological Other that supports the system as a whole. According to Žižek, it is precisely this sense of a big Other that, in the words of Matthew Sharpe, "is always *performatively presupposed* by interpellated subjects *in* their continuing self-identification within the given social order."[7] In other words, one is induced into ideological configurations by the continuing desire for an anchor to meaning that is then reified through the autonomous collective. Hence any critique of ideology involves the suspension of the big Other as the locus of support, repeating Christ's cry of dereliction, and thereby constituting a kind of *imitatio Christi*.

Belief before Belief

Žižek's debt to Althusser helps to highlight the radically exterior role Žižek ascribes to belief: belief is maintained not in Protestant terms as a passionately held viewpoint, but through the material practice of reli-

7. Matthew Sharpe, *Slavoj Žižek: A Little Piece of the Real* (Aldershot: Ashgate, 2004), p. 48.

gion. This is a feature of belief that Žižek returns to again and again, often arriving at it through varying viewpoints or examples, and offering various refinements in one way or another.

In *The Sublime Object of Ideology* he offers as examples the Tibetan prayer wheel: a prayer is written down, placed in a rotating drum, and spun almost automatically: the wheel prays for you (SOI, 34). Likewise, Christmas cards believe in Christmas for us; weepers cry at funerals in place of the mourners; and — to add to Žižek's list — candles continue to offer up a prayer for the parishioner who is free to return home. In short, it is not a question of believing *in* things, but of the things themselves believing for us (SOI, 34).

He also draws heavily on Octave Mannoni's work (FTKN, 245-49), and in particular "Je sais bien, mais quand même" ("I Know Quite Well but Still").[8] Mannoni's analysis of belief refers back to Freud's concept of neurotic disavowal *(Verleugnung)* as it arose in the context of castration. According to Freud, upon the sight of the vagina, and despite the obvious lack of penis, children are apt to "disavow the fact, and believe that they *do* see a penis," or that they see something small that will grow into a penis (SE, 19:143-44). Mannoni's point is that the mechanism of disavowal Freud initially discerned in children is indicative of the far more widespread way people maintain belief and ritual in their daily lives: we know it is not true, but nonetheless we continue to believe through the ritual. In short, all belief has the structure of neurotic disavowal.

This psychological account is further developed with reference to Lacan. In Seminar VII Lacan says the following regarding the role of the chorus in Greek tragedy: "When you go to the theatre in the evening, you are preoccupied by the affairs of the day, by the pen that you lost, by the cheque that you will have to sign the next day. You shouldn't give yourselves too much credit. Your emotions are taken charge of by the healthy order displayed on the stage. The Chorus takes care of them. The emotional commentary is done for you" (SVII, 252). Žižek finds here the precursor to canned laughter: canned laughter laughs for us, taking charge of our emotions after an exhausting day's work. Canned laughter is not a

---

8. Octave Mannoni, *Clefs pour l'Imaginaire ou l'Autre Scène* (Mayenne: Seuil, 1985), pp. 9-33.

prompt for us *to* laugh, it laughs in our place (ZR, 104). Drawing upon an intervention by Robert Pfaller (ZR, 123 n. 1), he refers to this more specifically as an example of "interpassivity," a point to be contrasted with "inter-active." Whereas with the latter the participant is active through the given media ("press the red button now!" etc.), interpassivity assumes that I am passive through another's activity.[9]

The interpassivity of belief, i.e., the distance between the believer and the ritual that sustains belief, is analogous in Lacanian terms to the gap between the subject of the statement and the subject of the enunciation (É, 677/800). The *subject of the statement* is the subject of the conscious dimension of speech; it "designates the subject insofar as he is currently speaking" (É, 677/800). In terms of Lacan's trinity, the subject of the statement corresponds to the symbolic. By contrast, *the subject of the enunciation* refers to the subject of the unconscious, discerned only in terms of "shifters," linguistic inflections that index but do not signify the subject. *The subject of the enunciation* corresponds to the real. Why the gap? Because as soon as we try to talk about ourselves, we turn ourselves into an object. As Lacan says in "Function and Field of Speech": "I identify myself in language, but only by losing myself in it as an object" (É, 247/299-300).

This is why Žižek says it is wrong to assume that one initially believes, only to then reify that belief through the material practice. Such an approach leaves intact the notion of the naive "one" who initially believed. By contrast: *"displacement is original and constitutive"* (PF, 108): there is no self-present being of whom belief could be dispossessed, because belief only arises in the gap.

One way to highlight the constitutive role of this gap in terms of be-

---

9. More recently Žižek has put forward an alternative approach with reference to Badiou: it may be "better to do nothing than engage in localised acts whose function is to make the system run smoother." In other words, the real threat to existing powers is not "passivity, but pseudo-activity" (e.g., the London peace march against the war on Iraq), an intervention that merely "masks the nothingness of what goes on." Hence the real challenge is precisely to step back and do nothing, to cultivate an "ominous passivity." Indeed, it might be added, was it not precisely this "ominous passivity" that characterized Christ's confrontation with the Roman authorities? Žižek, "Concesso non Dato," in *Traversing the Fantasy*, pp. 219-56, 253.

lief is to ask: What would it mean to believe *without* this minimal defense against the real of belief, to experience law (i.e., doctrine) not from the perspective of castration and hence lack, but in its pure immediacy? For Žižek this would be a traumatic encounter, an encounter with the zero-point of law, the point at which law is law not because it is grounded in some transcendental sense of the Good or the True, but because it is mercilessly imposed. In other words, it is unavoidable in the same way that to be a speaking being requires one to accept the traumatic imposition of the signifier, the cut or the Oedipal injunction. This is why rational argumentation for belief misses the point for Žižek. Belief evades rational judgment. In the end one simply believes unconditionally, an attitude that does not ask for legitimate reasons and for that very reason cannot be refuted (TS, 144). It is also why the criticism that Žižek's flirtation with theology risks the "irrationalism"[10] of unconditional faith misses the point: *there is no faith or belief, be it religious or secular, that is not in the final analysis unconditional,* i.e., simply accepted through the imposition of the signifier.

Little wonder, then, that in a more recent essay Žižek has fully embraced the logic of his own position: *I believe in order not to believe.*

> You find your belief too oppressing in its raw immediacy? Then kneel down, act as if you believed, and *you will get rid of your belief* — you will no longer have to believe yourself, your belief will already exist objectified in your act of praying. That is to say, what if one kneels down and prays not so much to regain one's own belief but, on the opposite, to *get rid* of one's belief, of its over-proximity, to acquire a breathing space of a minimal distance towards it? To believe — to believe directly, with out the externalising mediation of ritual — is a heavy, oppressive, traumatic burden.[11]

As strange as it seems, Žižek's position is entirely in keeping with the thought of Thomas Aquinas, the thirteenth-century Dominican. In reply

---

10. Geoff Boucher, "The Law as Thing: Žižek and the Graph of Desire," in *Traversing the Fantasy,* p. 44.

11. Žižek, "Concesso non Dato," p. 237.

to a question concerning the nature of ceremonial precepts (those acts that regulate worship), Aquinas begins by pointing out the difference between their function in the old and the new law. He makes the astonishing claim that "Just as human reason fails to grasp the import of poetical utterance on account of its deficiency in truth, neither can it grasp divine things perfectly on account of their superabundance of truth."[12] In other words, under the old law sacrifice was necessary because of the lack of truth; i.e., the "divine truth" had not been revealed through Christ.[13] But with the new law, ceremonial precepts are needed because the truth revealed through Christ is "superabundant [*excedentem*]."[14] It is as if, through Christ's revelation, the truth of God now shines so brightly in an ever unfolding and increasing measure that one needs the sacraments as a filter, like a pair of sunglasses, to funnel the divine radiance lest one burn one's eyes. In other words, contrary to the usual claim that the sacrifice offered at the altar ensures our community with God, Aquinas also suggests that the sacrifice at the altar ensures our distance *from* God; or rather, it ensures that any illumination received is in proper proportion to the capacities of the human intellect. To put it in Lacan's terms, Aquinas situates religion on the side of the symbolic and God on the side of the real. The sacraments are a defense against the real of God, establishing desire as a defense against his unbearable *jouissance.*

Returning to Ideology

Associating ideology with language and the symbolic in this way goes some way toward understanding how ideology maintains its grip. However, as Matthew Sharpe has argued, it suffers from two problems. First, it turns ideology into such a catchall phrase that it ceases to have any purchase;[15] second, it undercuts the ability for genuine critique. Regarding this latter point, Sharpe argues that Marx's critique of the political

---

12. *Summa Theologiæ* I-II, q. 101, a. 2, r. 2.

13. "It is only the truth of the glory to come, a truth not yet revealed, that has to be prefigured." *Summa Theologiæ* I-II, q. 101, a. 2, r. 2.

14. *Summa Theologiæ* I-II, q. 101, a. 2, r. 2.

15. Sharpe, *Slavoj Žižek,* p. 253.

economy was grounded in a properly dialectical critique; i.e., it took into account detailed analysis of the empirical systems of production and class antagonism. Hence, when it came to the question that Žižek's work on ideology champions: *What is to be done?* Marx was able to answer feasibly. In Žižek's work the problem arises because class antagonism is replaced by ontological antagonism, a dialectic between being (the symbolic) and nonbeing (the real). By situating the antagonism at the level of ontology, Žižek is thereby excused from "having to make any such arduous investigation of the 'empirical' intricacies of hegemonic order that he levels his critique at."[16]

Sharpe delineates the question well, but arguably is unable to provide the truly critical gesture, precisely because he is unable to offer up an alternate vision. The problem with Sharpe is that his criticism ("we need more empirical studies of the political machinations") fails to really take the question of ontology to account. Should one not question such foundational assumptions? After all, what is to stop our assumptions about ontology from governing the interpretation of empirical data?

Why Is the Something Nothing?

As Conor Cunningham has decisively shown, the ontological dialectic/antagonism that exists for Žižek between the symbolic and the real is but an example of a more pervasive *genealogy of nihilism*[17] where nihilism, or rather "philosophies of Nothing," is defined as the "sundering of the something, rendering it nothing, and then have the nothing be after all *as* something."[18] In short, nihilism involves having the Nothing as Something.

Cunningham's point is quite simple: many of our attempts to describe life end up destroying the thing in question by presupposing ab-

16. Sharpe, *Slavoj Žižek,* p. 253.

17. Conor Cunningham, *Genealogy of Nihilism* (London: Routledge, 2002), pp. 236-60; Cunningham, "Nothing Is, Something Must Be: Lacan and Creation from No One," in *Theology and the Political,* ed. Creston Davis, John Milbank, and Slavoj Žižek (Durham, N.C., and London: Duke University Press, 2005), pp. 72-101.

18. Cunningham, *Genealogy of Nihilism,* p. xiii.

sence beforehand. By way of example, one does well to recall Leonardo da Vinci's complaint that in drawing life he had first to rely on its death. Stealing cadavers from the local morgue, he would dissect them, peeling back the layers to observe the organs, muscles, and veins, through which life flowed. Hence, his anatomical sketches were not sketches of life, but of death. Therefore, in taking the drawings as depictions of life, we really have death *as* life, or in Cunningham's terms: the nothing as something.

This is the logic by which Cunningham identifies nihilism and its genealogy, which encompasses the history of Western philosophy. For example, Plotinus grounds being in nonbeing, Kant grounds the phenomena in the *noumenal*, Fichte grounds the I in Non-I, Derrida grounds the Text in Nothing, and Lacan grounds the symbolic in the unknowable *real*. In each case the logical status of the something (being, phenomena, a text, or a subject) is nothing because each rests upon its own absence.[19]

It is not difficult to recognize a series of dualisms here, yet as Cunningham argues, one should not be deceived. Each dualism rests within a monism, the difference within each dualism (presence/absence, text/void, etc.) being but a perspectival difference of a singular thing, i.e., the difference of a single thing seen from two different points, like Jastrow's duck/rabbit picture. One can see either one or the other, but not both at the same time, because the dualism is governed by a single picture. To employ Žižek's terms, one could speak of this perspectival difference in terms of the parallax view. For this reason, nihilism is unable to think genuine difference: difference is merely a gestalt effect like Jastrow's duck/rabbit picture. Moreover, because difference arises through a negation, it involves an inevitable violence, as indicated by Lacan: "the symbol first manifests itself as the killing of the thing" (É, 262/319).

Cunningham has given particular attention to Lacan and Žižek in his work. He asks: What are the relative positions of being and thought in their schemes? Lacan is clear on this point: "The discordance between knowledge and being is my subject" (SXX, 120). According to Lacan, one is faced with the *Vel* (the mathematical sign for an either/or choice) of alienation (SXI, 211). At the threshold of subjectivity one is faced with a

19. Cunningham, *Genealogy of Nihilism*, p. xii.

choice; one can either choose being and thereby disappear as subject (i.e., remain outside the sociosymbolic system and hence remain as nothing), or one can choose meaning (i.e., enter the symbolic, become a thinking subject) and survive, but only to "emerge in the field of the Other, to be in a large part of its field, eclipsed by the disappearance of being induced by the very function of the signifier" (SXI, 211).

Little wonder that Sharpe finds fault with Žižek's underlying ontology. The Lacanian subject is left to vacillate within this impossible monism, ever caught between being and meaning (thought), unable to make a progressive step beyond the critique.

The question arises for Cunningham: *Can there be a nonreductive and nonviolent community between being and thought?* The strength of Cunningham's approach is not simply to oppose theology to nihilism as the great panacea, but rather to show the proximity between the two, to show how Christianity is *already* a form of nihilism — nihilism from an alternative perspective. After all, is not creation ex nihilo the proto-form of nihilism: From the nothing issues something? There remains, however, a crucial distinction. In its secular form, nihilism construes the lack as privation, i.e., something violently withheld as the very condition of subjectivity, what Freud called castration. Hence lack is primarily an absence of something. And it is for this reason that thought or language necessarily falls short for Lacan and Žižek. This is the lack as scarcity — not unlike the way prices are artificially inflated through the withholding of goods in the economic sphere.

Theology, by contrast, starts from the primacy of gift. This is not to say that we as creatures treat creation primarily as a gift — such an approach leaves intact the notion of the subject as well as privileging reception over gift. Rather, we ourselves *are* this very gift, already begun. From this perspective "Nothing" changes and hence *everything* changes. Where lack was conceived of as a scarcity, it is now possible to conceive it from the perspective of divine plenitude. This in turn allows for an affirmation of the material world not present in Lacan and Žižek. As Cunningham explains:

> We return to the object because it calls us again, and we have forgotten the hue of its beauty, for we cannot quite recall the plenitude of its

form; is such a non-identical repetition not the only way to return to the face of our lover? Indeed, is this not the rich thrust of desire, one that keeps pulling us back to the very depth of the surface? Consequently, the phenomenological resistance we meet in the handshake or in intercourse, is not to be read as a failure of intimacy; resistance being read as an excluding distance. For such resistance does not mock our efforts to encounter; indeed, the logic that generates such an understanding is governed by a vicious idealism that hates the body, which it deems a creation of Satan, and which it seeks to destroy. . . . In returning to the object we answer a call — this is our calling — doing so with the offer of a hopeful name; and we are called by a name that we too exceed. In this way, being is not beyond thought; it is the beyond *of* thought.[20]

To repeat, being is not by necessity *alienated* from thought; nonetheless, it is the beyond of thought. Hence our failed relations to the material world need not be seen in terms of a Gnostic rejection of bodily creation, but as a sign that our telos lays beyond ourselves, that we are already thought and hence self-transcending. Cunningham is not therefore reducing being to thought as if his work were driven by the register of the imaginary. Nor is he setting one over and against the other in the manner of Lacan and Žižek. Rather, he is offering the *properly paradoxical* position — a more immanent account of immanence — whereby it is precisely through recourse to the beyond of thought, induced by God, as it were, that one gains a deeper understanding of the surface (i.e., material existence). In other words, contrary to the usual argument that Christianity is world-denying, pinning all its hopes in the afterlife — Nietzsche's critique of Christianity[21] — it is only by affirming this metalevel that one validates the material world.[22]

20. Cunningham, *Genealogy of Nihilism*, p. 260.
21. "In God a declaration of hostility towards life, nature, the will-to life!" F. Nietzsche, *Twilight of the Idols/The Anti-Christ*, trans. R. Hollingdale (London: Penguin Books, 2003), p. 140.
22. Cunningham, *Genealogy of Nihilism*, p. 177.

ŽIŽEK

Nihilism and Castration

This shift from *lack as privation* to *lack as plenitude* was already anticipated by Lacan in his distinction between the masculine and feminine positions of sexuation (see chapter 4). Masculinity is marked by the lack that accompanies castration: in the economy of enjoyment *(jouissance)* something is always held back. By contrast, Lacan argued that woman is *"not* not at all there. She is there in full *(à plein).* But there is something more *(en plus)"* (SXX, 74). This is not to say that woman is not castrated, but that castration is not a singular trait that defines all women in the way it does for men. When it comes to the clinic and the complaints of men, there is a single condition for men. Women by contrast can only ever be treated in singular terms because they have something more. If one is left wanting in the face of a woman, it is not because she is lacking something; it is because her plenitude exposes the lack in man.

One can extend the comparison. Nihilism conforms to the logic of masculinity to the extent that it mythically reconstructs the logic of the primal murder (i.e., castration). On the basis of Darwin's work, Freud put forward the bold thesis that the father of a primal horde (the alpha male) was killed and eaten by his sons as a means for them to gain access to the women (i.e., an unbounded *jouissance).* However, the ensuing guilt led to the establishment of the twin Oedipal laws: the law against murder and the law of exogamy. And it was in the enactment of these laws that culture and religion were born (SE, 13:141-42). Nihilism repeats this myth through the logic of a founding negation as constitutive of the social whole: the void that stands as the condition of law. In other words, nihilism is the philosophical equivalent of the law of castration. By contrast, Nietzsche was right: Christianity is a woman, it harbors the principle of divine plenitude of which nihilism knows nothing.[23]

Reading nihilism this way also underlines Cunningham's point that nihilism is unable to generate difference, because according to Lacan, the logic of masculinity is the logic of homogeneity. All men are the same (i.e., they come under the law of castration), although there remains one exception — the primal father. By contrast, woman can be treated only in

23. Nietzsche, *Twilight of the Idols/The Anti-Christ,* p. 50.

68

the singular, and hence woman is the principle of difference. In this sense, difference is comprised of each addition, rather than resolved into universal logic.

The Excremental Remainder

Žižek's nihilism is further highlighted by his pejorative use of the *real*. As Cunningham observes, Žižek "display[s] a lust for the void based on the excremental horror he claims to discern in life's excess: the excess which life is."[24] For Žižek the excess of life returns not as divine plenitude, the original goodness of abundant difference, but as an overwhelming sense of the void. The *something more* that characterizes desire is not identifiable as a positive entity; rather, it is experienced as the immanent inertia that sits at the intersection between the material and symbolic worlds. Despite its negative quality, Lacan is able to say: "the real is full";[25] not in the sense that that real has been "filled up," but that through its very negativity it is able to permeate experience, not unlike how silence can be deafening. In other words, the very absence itself becomes the source of abundance.

Two issues are at stake in all this. First, a failure to think the material, i.e., an inability by Žižek to affirm the priority of something over the nothing. Second, where the "presymbolic" is felt in its negativity, it is always excremental, i.e., impure or unaffirmed in its ontological goodness. Regarding the first, it should be noted that despite Žižek's criticisms of the "Gnostic dream of the immaterial" (OB, 33-35), he retains just such a Neoplatonic shift *away* from matter to the immateriality of the sign. This makes a lie of his "materialist" theology; there is no materiality, only the negativity of the *real*, i.e., the body, present only in its absence, and which over and against stands the symbolic. The irony of this should not be lost: Žižek's abandonment of the onto-theological God in favor of a moment of absolute dereliction — absolute in the sense that abandonment

---

24. Cunningham, *Genealogy of Nihilism*, p. 258.

25. Lacan, in Anthony Wilden, *The Language of the Self* (Baltimore: Johns Hopkins University Press, 1968), p. 271.

ŽIŽEK

has the last word — does not result in a materialist theology, but in the inverse, an idealist and Gnostic philosophy.

Against this one can pit the argument of Catherine Pickstock. She maintains that it is not difficult to read Plato's theory of the forms as leading to a denigration of the material and temporal world (i.e., the sensible world) in favor of the real word (i.e., the supersensible), where Goodness, Truth, and Beauty reside, untouched by the contingent and therefore inferior realm of matter, the Sophistic and Neoplatonic reading. Yet it is also possible to read Plato from another position, the key to which lies in *participation (methexis)*. As she explains: "Plato portrays the transcendence of the good, its beyond presence-and-absence, as a kind of *contagion,* for its plenitude spills over into immanence, in such a way that the good is revealed in the beauty of physical particulars."[26] In other words, the forms spill over, giving the material world a dignity precisely because in the encounter with something of beauty one *participates* in something of the divine. Thus, far from Platonic metaphysics devaluing the sensible order, it fundamentally affirms it. As James Smith puts it, "The philosopher sees 'through' the material to the transcendent, whereas in fact it is the sophist who reduces the sensible to the merely immanent."[27] One could say that Žižek repeats the sophistry of old to the extent that he denies the genuine apprehension of the physical world while reducing the transcendent to the immanent.

John Milbank has suggested that the material element to Christianity goes some way in explaining the theological turn among the neo-Lacanians, including Žižek, Alain Badiou, and more recently Peter Hallward: "because this discourse alone permits an ideal materialism that does not result in an out-and-out triumph of Idealism."[28] In other words, the postmetaphysical turn has not shifted the philosophical emphasis away from the abstract to a bodily informed practice but the inverse: it has resulted in a shift away from the body; and the theological turn testifies to this need, it "fleshes out" their work. The problem with

26. Catherine Pickstock, *After Writing: On the Liturgical Consummation of Philosophy* (Oxford: Blackwell, 1998), p. 12.

27. James Smith, *Speech and Theology: Language and the Logic of Incarnation* (London and New York: Routledge, 2002), p. 174.

28. Milbank, "Materialism and Transcendence," in *Theology and the Political,* p. 402.

Žižek's work, therefore, is not that it is *too* Christian à la Parker, but that it is *not* Christian enough. By maintaining recourse to the transcendent, one can paradoxically affirm the goodness of the material world, an affirmation without which materiality risks evaporating back into the nothing.

Regarding the second point (i.e., the presymbolic is always excremental), as Cunningham suggests referring to Johann Georg Hamann (1730-88), one of the prime movers of the Sturm und Drang movement, "all that is made is clean, in so far as what God makes is clean, so we must not call it profane. Indeed, according to Christianity, God became man and so He had genitalia, bowel movements and so on."[29] Consequently, Christianity rejoices in the body. Moreover, as Cunningham says, "just because that which manifests itself escapes our categories (appearing ugly) to dismiss it as horrible is to remain reactively constituted by an idealism that displays a distinct lack of *caritas*."[30]

Such distrust echoes the liberal suspicion upon which the social is grounded. According to the early theorists of liberalism such as Thomas Hobbes, man, when left to a state of nature, was a self-seeking individual who acted to preserve his own. The presumption here is that nature is primarily a state of warring chaos. Nonetheless, it was argued that man also contained the faculty of reason to which one could appeal. Hence the case was made that by ceding some rights in the social arena, coming together through a social contract of sorts, one could prevent the descent into "the war of all against all." Such a viewpoint suggests not only that the social is primarily a suspended violence, but also that every other is to be treated first and foremost as a threat. For Žižek it is the real of existence that is perceived primarily in terms of a threat, and hence he refuses to assert its goodness through the primacy of *caritas*. Yet, as Milbank argues in *Theology and Social Theory*, there is no reason to suggest that the will to power (i.e., action predicated upon self-interest) is any more primary than the will to *caritas*, and hence the possibility of an initial affirmation of the goodness of creation that precedes its overall threat.

29. Cunningham, *Genealogy of Nihilism*, p. 258.
30. Cunningham, *Genealogy of Nihilism*, p. 259.

Returning to Sharpe's initial criticism — Žižek's ontology is unable to sustain a positive program of engagement for the Left — it can be argued that theology offers an alternative ontology. On the one hand, it affirms a material basis for such a program because it does not consign critique to a tragic identification with the void. It assumes instead the priority of presence. On the other hand, Christian ontology refuses the liberal suspicion of the other in favor of the primacy of *caritas,* the charitable action upon which revolution may be predicated. This is also why the standard criticism that Žižek's theological turn risks propagating an uncritical and irrational faith — easily identifiable with today's fundamentalist religious groups or political absolutism — misses the mark. Given the normativity of secular nihilism, the truly critical gesture is to suspend nihilism itself and make a wager on matter — the stuff of creation.

CHAPTER 3

Why the Political Act Must Necessarily Adopt the Form of the Religious Act

In an interview with *Radical Philosophy* back in 1991, Žižek explained something of the political background informing his early work. On the one hand there was a rising trend of nationalism that in nearby Serbia was given brutal expression in Slobodan Milosevic's drive to rid the area of ethnic Albanians; on the other hand there was the unfettered embrace of market liberalism. Opposition was to be found in what Žižek describes as an "old New Left," a liberal voice connected to the new social causes such as peace or human rights, committed all the while to a political critique of the economy. Žižek was instrumental in formally establishing such an opposition (TS, 207-8), going on to stand as a Liberal candidate in Slovenia's first free elections. Speaking then, he outlined his political position: "What defines the distinctive role of the Liberal Party is our opposition to the rise of this national-organic-populism in Slovenia. . . . Our aim is to promote pluralism, and an awareness of ecological issues, and to defend the rights of minorities. This is the kind of liberal tradition we represent. Not the purely capitalist values of the free market."[1] Since then, the emphasis in Žižek's work has fallen away from the rights of minorities or peace activism, toward the political critique of the economy and "the burning question of how we are to reformulate a leftist, anti-capitalist political project in our era of global capitalism" (TS, 4). How does one account for this shift? The problem arises for Žižek be-

---

1. Žižek, "Lacan in Slovenia: An Interview with Slavoj Žižek and Renata Salecl," *Radical Philosophy* 58 (1991): 25-31, 28.

cause, first, the rights of minorities can easily translate into identity politics whereby the task is simply to further the interests of particular groups or individuals on the basis of a supposed identity such as religion, gender, disability, or race, rather than challenging the economic system as a whole. In short, the Left was losing its radicalism. Second: given that capitalism has achieved hegemony to the extent that "we silently assume that the liberal-democratic global order is somehow the finally found 'natural' social regime" (FA, 10), there is a renewed task to articulate an alternative.

Given this state, any kind of political intervention cannot be simply a matter of exposing the injustice of the prevailing order; after all, any such criticism can easily be accommodated back into the system — for example, some extra spending here or increased awareness there. Rather, what is required is a *radical break,* a gesture that brings the system as a whole into question. Žižek calls this the politics of the *act,* a radical politics. To clarify this point he refers to the distinction between politics and the political: "'politics' *qua* separate social complex, positively determined subsystem of social relations in interaction with other subsystems (economy, forms of culture . . .), and 'the Political *(le Polititque)*' *qua* the moment of openness, of undecidability, when the very structuring principle of society, the fundamental form of the social pact, is called into question — in short, the moment of global crisis overcome by the act of founding 'new harmony.'"[2] It is not difficult to see here the contribution psychoanalysis has to make in this regard. On the one hand it lends itself to Marx's theory of ideology, providing a more nuanced working of our psychological attachments to those regulative systems and subsystems of power that structure our everyday lives, i.e., how we are unconsciously interpellated through ritual actions into the symbolic universe. On the other hand it offers a model for radical intervention, an attempt to suspend the laws or fantasies that structure neurotic repetition, not merely at the level of existing social relations, but the entire social field itself, because an act must break with all existing codes. One

---

2. Žižek, "Why Should a Dialectician Learn to Count to Four?" *Radical Philosophy* 58 (1991): 3-9, 8. Žižek is drawing here upon the work of Claude Lefort, *The Political Forms of Modern Society* (Cambridge: Polity, 1986), and Ernesto Laclau, *New Reflections on the Revolution of Our Time* (London: Verso, 1990).

can readily see therefore, as Žižek does, the link between the political agent and the analysand. A political agent, like the analysand, has to commit an act that can be authorized only by him, an act for which there is no external guarantee.

However, as I argue in this chapter, what is missing from this account is the central role played by theology. Why theology? First: as a matter of *convenientia,* or "fittingness." If Marxism requires a supplementary science of the psyche, then surely, as Lacan would argue, it also requires a third category to triangulate the other two and complete the trinity: the symbolic (sociology), the imaginary (psychology), and the real (theology). Second: because theology has been historically formative in the formulation of Lacan's thought, not simply for the obvious reason that Christian thought has been formative throughout Western culture, but for reasons particular to the climate of French thought. During Lacan's early years (1930s to 1950s) French Jesuits and Dominicans instigated a *ressourcement,* a return to the patristic sources of theology to recover a paradoxical understanding of subjectivity. This was to have a profound influence on French cultural life and beyond — feeding directly into the reforms of Vatican II. My argument in this chapter is that Lacan's return to Freud was an instance of this theological *ressourcement.* Third: because in recovering the theological underpinnings of these debates it is possible to move beyond the impasse of Žižek's work, which I identify as *transgression without progression,* i.e., a revolutionary act that is unable to sustain itself as anything other than a moment of profound rupture.

In the final part of the chapter I respond to Žižek's claim that the political act requires an ahistorical kernel of historicity, something outside the normal ebb and flow of historical succession that proves constitutive of genuine historical and political change. I argue that the incarnation is that ahistorical kernel by which history is constituted par excellence, and hence Christianity the condition of the political act, a point made excellently by Kierkegaard. And because Christ serves as the condition of the act, yet opens out into liturgical repetition, it offers a model of *transgression with progression.* I begin, however, by turning to the work of Alain Badiou, whose work has been decisive for Žižek's articulation of the political act.

ŽIŽEK

Badiou *avec* Saint Paul

In developing the category of the act, Žižek has drawn extensively upon the work of Alain Badiou, and in particular Badiou's militant and materialist reading of Saint Paul. Badiou is himself clearly indebted to Lacan, whom he affectionately refers to as "our Hegel."[3] And so it is helpful in presenting the political act to refer directly back to Badiou's text and his formulation of the political act.

As Theodore Jennings, Jr., has pointed out, until Badiou's book *Saint Paul,* work on Paul's letters tended to serve either confessional groups or theologians working in areas of scriptural, historical, or dogmatic questions. Moreover, exegesis has tended to be largely Protestant to the extent that it has stressed justification through faith. Therefore, on the question of political/social injustice or wrongdoing of a sort, one was always referred back to the interior: one transforms one's personal relation to the divine and hopes that social transformation will follow. Hence the primacy of Paul's political contribution was overlooked in favor of a right relation with God.[4]

By contrast, Badiou uses Paul's letter to the Romans as a formal description of the process by which a universal truth is arrived at. Paul is held up as an example of a radical militant who makes the absolute break with all that went before. What is at stake in Badiou's description has nothing to do with what Paul *actually* says (i.e., the content of his letters), any more than whether Christianity is *actually* true. Instead, Badiou is concerned with the formal procedure of truth as it relates to the birth of Christianity; in other words, how a truth is universally established.

At this point one should clarify what Badiou means by truth. To borrow from Peter Hallward's succinct summary: "what Badiou calls a truth is the process that, sparked by a break with routine, persists as an affirmation whose progressive imposition transforms the very way things *appear* in the situation."[5] On this account truth does not concern the

3. J. Barker, *Alain Badiou: A Critical Introduction* (London: Pluto, 2002), p. 2.

4. Theodore Jennings, Jr., *Reading Derrida/Thinking Paul* (Stanford: Stanford University Press, 2006), pp. 1-2.

5. Peter Hallward, ed., *Think Again: Alain Badiou and the Future of Philosophy* (London: Continuum, 2004), p. 2.

correspondence between knowledge and its object, as if reality itself had been given in advance and all one had to do was discover it or ensure the right representation thereof. Truth is a process, a dynamic operation; truth does not describe the world as real, it *creates* it as real by retroactively transforming the past to give meaningfulness to the present.

The truth process begins properly with an "unpredictable encounter," a break *(trauma)* or moment of grace within the existing order that "escapes conventional representation."[6] Badiou often uses the example of an amorous encounter that has the power to change one's life. In *Saint Paul: The Foundation of Universalism,* it is Paul's claim that "Christ is resurrected" that escapes all previous logic. Badiou calls this irruption an "event." An event cannot belong to a given situation, nor can it be interpreted in terms of existing ideologies; if it were, it would not constitute something new. Instead, an event gives rise to something new altogether. In the case of Paul, the claim "Christ is resurrected" breaks with the existing background of Greek philosophy or Jewish legalism: Christianity introduces something wholly *new.* Again, what matters is not whether Christ was *actually* resurrected but the eventful nature of the declaration itself, unspoiled by any knowledge of the historical Jesus, standing instead for the subjective possibility of victory over death. In this way Badiou's account recalls the disregard Paul has for Christ in Martin Scorsese's *Last Temptation of Christ,* based upon the novel by Nikos Kazantzakis. Christ's last temptation is to climb down from the cross, to relinquish himself of his messianic task and pursue instead a domestic life including marriage to Mary Magdalene with whom he will have children. It is in his capacity as a normal man that he subsequently encounters Paul preaching the resurrection. Upon challenging Paul with the claim that he did not resurrect, Paul says, "Look at all these people, look at their faces. Do you see how unhappy they are? . . . Their only hope is the resurrected Jesus. . . . I don't care whether you are Jesus or not, the resurrected Jesus will save the world."[7] In short, what matters is not the literal truth of the resurrection, but the way one is carried through fidelity to the event that subsequently establishes it

---

6. Hallward, *Think Again,* p. 3.

7. *The Last Temptation of Christ,* directed by Martin Scorsese (1989) (Universal Pictures, Universal Studios, 1998), DVD.

as a universal field of truth — universal in the sense that it defines the field itself. And it is precisely fidelity to the event that gives rise to the process of subjectivization, i.e., becoming an apostle: "The apostle is then he who names this possibility (the Gospels, the Good News, comes down to this: we 'can' vanquish death). His discourse is one of pure fidelity to the possibility opened up by the event.... It cannot, therefore, in any way ... fall under the remit of knowledge. The philosopher knows eternal truth; the prophet knows the univocal sense of what will come.... The apostle, who declares an unheard-of possibility, one dependant on an eventual grace, properly speaking knows nothing."[8]

In other words, truth begins with a wager, a formal decision upon something that is neither calculable nor demonstrable, and for which the results cannot be known in advance, but to which the subject declares his faith; in the act of faith the subject gives fixity to the event. Thereafter the process of truth becomes one of infinite verification, i.e., a constant examination within the situation of the consequences of the wager upon which the event was initially decided. That is to say, truth persists "insofar as these implications can be upheld in rigorously universal terms, i.e. in terms that relate to all members of their situation *without* passing through the prevailing criteria of recognition, classification and domination which underlie the normal organization of that situation."[9]

Henceforth Christianity cannot be judged true by external criteria (e.g., is there really a God?), but by whether its participants maintain fidelity to the event of the resurrection in such a way that it organizes a new field of experience.

It is not difficult to feel here the Kierkegaardian resonance to Badiou's work, as Žižek himself points out.

> Badiou's notion of subjectivisation as the engagement on behalf of Truth, as fidelity to the Truth-Event is clearly indebted to the Kierkegaardian existential commitment experienced as gripping our whole being. Political and religious movements can grip us in this way, as

8. Alain Badiou, *Saint Paul: The Foundation of Universalism*, trans. R. Brassier (Stanford: Stanford University Press, 2003), p. 45.

9. Hallward, *Think Again*, p. 3, italics mine.

can love relationships and, for certain people, such "vocations" as science and art. When we respond to such a summons with what Kierkegaard calls infinite passion — that is, when we respond by accepting an unconditional commitment — this commitment determines what will be the significant issue for us for the rest of our life.[10]

Indeed, one way to describe his project is as the most concerted attempt yet to politicize Kierkegaard, i.e., to translate the question of faith and commitment into political terms. According to Kierkegaard, the paradox of Christianity is that it invites one to make a decision about one's eternal happiness based upon a historical and contingent event: that God entered time in the form of the incarnation. The problem arises because the gap between the two — the historical point of departure and eternal happiness — is incommensurate. If one takes the objective standpoint, waiting for historical evidence or some sort of proof as such, one ends up indefinably postponing what is arguably the most important decision one could make, a decision about one's eternal happiness. If one is to make a commitment, therefore, one can do so only through an act of faith. The twist is that the very gap of incommensurability between the two means one cannot make the leap lightly. Instead, one must leap with earnestness toward the absolute, the very risk of the venture thereby cultivating an inward and existential passion for God: "Faith is the contradiction between the infinite passion of inwardness and the objective uncertainty. If I am able to comprehend God objectively, I do not have faith; but because I cannot do this, I must have faith. If I want to keep myself in faith, I must continually see to it that I hold fast the objective uncertainty, see to it that in the objective uncertainty I am 'out on 70,000 fathoms of water' and still have faith."[11]

This is an "extreme" Christianity, predicated upon risk and passion in which one is suspended above the depths without rational support, maintained only by the passion of the commitment. There is a moment of madness here: one wagers one's eternal happiness on an event that de-

10. Žižek, "What If the Other Is Stupid?" in *Think Again,* p. 256 n. 8.

11. Kierkegaard, *Concluding Unscientific Postscript,* vol. 1, trans. H. Hong and E. Hong (Princeton: Princeton University Press, 1992), p. 204.

fies rational mediation, essentially risking all for something that remains unknown; yet as Kierkegaard points out, were one to adopt the objective standpoint, one would inevitably postpone the question of one's eternal happiness, forever waiting upon some new piece of scientific, textual, or archaeological evidence.

Badiou's work on Paul and truth is closely related to his political thought. What does Badiou understand by politics? To borrow again from Hallward's succinct summary: "True politics is a matter of collective mobilization guided by a general will . . . and not the business of bureaucratic administration (i.e. lobbying for funds, distribution of wealth etc.) or the socialised negotiation of interests (i.e. representing the people)."[12] Politics involves a collective wager upon an uncertainty, through which a new order can arise. Like Žižek's work, what is at stake here is politics as a critical gesture, a gesture that cannot simply be subsumed back into the prevailing order, but one that establishes a new field of reference in its entirety.

As the subtitle to *Saint Paul: The Foundation of Universalism* suggests, Badiou shares with Žižek a distrust of postmodern multiculturalism, championing instead a new universalism. Why universalism? What is at stake here is the way the truth process opens up a situation that transcends differences precisely to the extent that the situation renders them void. In other words, something is universal if it is beyond established differences. Although Paul recognizes the difference between Jews and Greeks, nonetheless in Christ one exceeds those differences, moving beyond them ("In Christ there is neither Jew nor Greek"). It is not that one is called to renounce one's previous customs, but more simply, those marks of difference cease to play a determinate role regarding one's identity. For this reason Paul does not discriminate either for or against circumcision; in the light of the Christ event, circumcision simply ceases to matter. Badiou thereby offers a voluntarist account of universalism. Universals are not universal in the Platonic sense, i.e., a transcendental form in which one participates such that any experienced beauty necessarily participates in its universal form. Rather, the event allows for a universal situation to arise precisely to the extent that through passion-

12. Hallward, *Think Again*, p. 3.

ate commitment (i.e., an act of will) what went before has no subsequent holding upon the situation.

Žižek and Badiou

In an interview with Joshua Delpech-Ramey, Žižek makes the following criticism of Badiou's project: Badiou's work separates out life from death, privileging the former at the expense of the latter. As Žižek says:

> Christ's death is not in itself the Truth-Event, it simply prepares the site for the Event (resurrection) by asserting the identity of God and Man — the fact that the infinite dimension of Immortal Truth is also accessible to the human finite mortal; what ultimately matters is only the resurrection of the dead Christ signalling that each human being can be redeemed and can enter the domain of Eternal Life, that is, participate in the Truth-Event. (TS, 147)

Although I am also taking St. Paul as a model, a formal structure which can then be applied to revolutionary emancipatory collectivities, and so on, nonetheless I try to ground it in a specific Christian content, which again for me focuses precisely on Christ's death, [his] death and resurrection. I am trying even to identify the two. The idea that resurrection follows death, the idea that these are two narrative events, this is at the narrative level of what Hegel would have called *vorstellungen,* representations. Actually, the two of them are even united. That is to say that Christ's death, in the Hegelian reading, is the disappearance of disappearance. It is in itself already what becomes for itself the new community.[13]

Žižek's criticism here is that Badiou focuses on the resurrection to the exclusion of death. But why should the negative gesture be so crucial? In *The Ticklish Subject,* Žižek explains:

13. An interview with Slavoj Žižek, "On Divine Self-Limitation and Revolutionary Love," *Journal of Philosophy and Scripture;* http://www.philosophyandscripture.org/ Issue1-2/Slavoj_Žižek/slavoj_Žižek.html (accessed August 16, 2007).

For Lacan, negativity, a negative gesture of withdrawal, precedes any positive gesture of enthusiastic identification with a Cause: negativity functions as the condition of (im)possibility of the enthusiastic identification — that is to say, it lays the ground, opens up space for it, but is simultaneously obfuscated by it and undermines it. For this reason, Lacan implicitly changes the balance between Death and Resurrection in favour of Death: what "Death" stands for at its most radical is not merely the passing of earthly life, but the "night of the world," the self-withdrawal, the absolute contraction of subjectivity, the severing of its links with "reality" — *this* is the "wiping the slate clean" that opens up the domain of the symbolic New Beginning, of the emergence of the "New harmony" sustained by a newly emerged Master-Signifier. (TS, 154)

In other words, negativity is the constitutive moment of the act, without which the act cannot take place. This is what it means to *traverse the fantasy:* to embrace the negativity that arises in the destruction of one's symbolic supports so that one might act in a way not circumscribed by neurotic identification or existing ideology. And this is why resurrection is identifiable with death.

Žižek's contention here is not a criticism of Badiou in toto; he remains within the terms of the debate. His point is simply that what is lost in Badiou's emphasis on resurrection is death. And herein lies the problem: he accepts the coordinates of the debate, failing to challenge Badiou's approach as a whole, adopting instead a crude Protestant disruption between nature and grace, such that one is always set in opposition to the other; hence the only politics possible is a politics of transgression, and not the progressive vision of socialism.

In what follows I submit that a return to the scholastic sources of Lacan brings to light an alternative logic, arguably a more Catholic logic that addresses this problem by pointing to God's self-revelation in the world, and through Christ as the ahistorical kernel of historicity, thereby refusing the possibility of total abandonment as the basis of the political act. In other words, the scholastic tradition offers a truly redemptive politics because it does not construe life in terms of a broken world that can be overturned only by a rupture of grace, i.e., the event, but a world already graced and participatory in God. In fashioning my argument I draw initially upon John Milbank's influential critique of Žižek in which the scholastic terms of the debate are first introduced.

Milbank and Žižek: Socialism and Scholasticism

As Richard Johnson has suggested, the thrust of Milbank's criticism can be profitably explored by way of the distinction that arose during the Enlightenment between negative and positive accounts of freedom. According to the former type, championed by the English philosopher J. S. Mill, among others, freedom is primarily freedom *from* the state or religion, etc., i.e., the freedom to pursue one's self-interest without the intervention of others. According to the latter model, championed by Rousseau and others, freedom is the freedom *to* pursue what one naturally is. Further to Rousseau's account is the distinction he draws between the will-of-all and the general will. The will-of-all refers to a consensus arrived at through the calculated interest of individuals, and hence represents a somewhat artificial consensus. But where people are encouraged to vote on the basis of what they think is sincerely beneficial as a whole, Rousseau held, the general will arises, a kind of natural law that gives expression to the Good. In developing a socialist ontology, Milbank clearly privileges the latter, although not without serious qualification.[14] For example, he says: "socialism requires our solidarity in the name of a positive affirmation of life and its plenitude."[15] He resists situating socialism within formal and rationalist elements of the Enlightenment, arguing instead that it arose with "*counter*-Enlightenment elements following the collapse of the hopes of the French Revolution: it was concerned with reestablishing, albeit in a more egalitarian mode, bonds of fraternity and

14. Milbank rejects Rousseau's liberalism: "[The] defence of the absolute sovereignty of the general will as grounded in a particular legal framework which guaranteed a freedom for the individual subject so long as it did not interfere with the freedom of others." Milbank, *Theology and Social Theory*, 2nd ed. (Oxford: Blackwell, 2006), p. 63.

15. Milbank, "Materialism and Transcendence," in *Theology and the Political: The New Debate*, ed. C. Davis, J. Milbank, and S. Žižek (Durham, N.C., and London: Duke University Press, 2005), p. 399.

solidarity which transcend a mere formulistic respect for freedom [i.e., a negative freedom] . . . , and was grounded in a shared vision of the substantive Good which the first socialists often assumed would be a religious one, expressed in some form of religious practice."[16] Given the seeming demise of religion in the West along with socialism, Milbank goes on to say: "We are now bound to ask whether capitalism is not the definitive shape of secularity, and whether by contrast community is not an intrinsically religious, mythical matter, so that with the demise of common belief, only a competitive market system in all spheres can organise and manage the resultant pursuit of remorseless self-interest by individuals."[17]

How does this relate to Žižek? Milbank's initial contention is that Žižek's work places undue emphasis on the negative to the extent that it undermines the positive base required of socialism. For example, in Žižek's work, relations are always relations of lack, constituted speculatively, which, as I argued in chapter 1, promotes the status of victimhood. Likewise, in regard to desire, it is always predicated upon a lack and hence in the final analysis always refers to the impossible object. And because one can never be rid of impossible desire, one can easily imagine the gesture of revolution (e.g., the suspension of law), but not the progressive path toward socialism.[18] Indeed, Žižek concedes as much when he says: "Lacan's way is not that of St. Paul" because psychoanalysis does not "posit a 'new harmony' . . . it — as it were — merely wipes the slate clean for one" (TS, 153). In other words, Lacanian analysis offers no positive prescription, such as a just law or a just desire. Hence Milbank contends that "the problem is not that the new Lacanian-Leninist revolutionary may will dubious means toward a just end, but rather that he or she may conceive no innately just."[19] Because, according to Milbank, socialism is not about discovering alternative economic models to combat poverty or social injustice, but is an attempt to fulfill people in aesthetic, ethical, and contemplative ways.

16. Milbank, *Being Reconciled: Ontology and Pardon* (London: Routledge, 2003), pp. 162-63.

17. Milbank, *Being Reconciled*, p. 163.

18. Milbank, "Materialism and Transcendence," p. 421.

19. Milbank, "Materialism and Transcendence," p. 422.

To revive the possibility of a more substantial critique that moves beyond the gesture of revolution, one needs to take into account the work of the French Jesuit Henri de Lubac. De Lubac was among the group of Jesuits who spearheaded the *ressourcement* (return to the sources) theology of the 1930s to 1950s — the first in a succession of "returns" that characterized French intellectual life and of which Lacan provides an exemplary example. The influence of these theological debates on French culture and in particular on Lacan (and by extension Žižek) should not be overlooked. What was at stake was the traditionalism and universalism of the Catholic Church against cultural modernism and historical relativism, and the inadequacy of the former to provide a response to the latter. The results of these debates would lead directly to the monumental reforms of Vatican II.

The irony was that those leading the reforms, such as de Lubac, were the very ones calling for a return to the sources. What, then, was the nature of their return? First, it was a return to the patristic and medieval sources of the church, especially Augustine and Aquinas; second, it was a return in the sense of a renewal, discovered through careful readings of the texts, with attention to translations and the immediate historical and theological context. This was a radical departure from the way Aquinas had been understood or taught in the seminaries. Up to that point his reception had relied heavily upon commentators such as Cardinal Cajetan (1465-1534) and Francisco Suárez (1548-1617).

Cajetan read Aquinas in terms of a crude dualism between nature and grace. So, given Aquinas's axioms *gratia praesupponit naturam* (grace presupposes or builds on nature) and *gratia perficit naturam* (grace perfects nature),[20] the working assumption is that man occupies a realm of nature, to which is added some extra and extrinsic supernature, a position later called extrinsicism. This was not without some theological justification; the impetus lay in the need to establish a realm of pure nature, independent of God, such that God's love could be gratuitously given. But in doing so Cajetan began to untie the paradoxical unity that underlined Aquinas's thought according to which humans were already graced with a natural desire *for* the supernatural (paradoxical because the end exceeds

---

20. *Summa Theologiæ* I, q. 2, a. 2.

its beginning). Moreover, as de Lubac notes, it is a short step from a realm of "pure nature" to a thoroughgoing naturalism after which it becomes difficult to see why recourse to a higher God is necessary.

Suárez's approach was to bring Aquinas into line with other scholastics such as Bonaventure and Duns Scotus, so as to present a unified and perennial philosophical system, which, from our present perspective, can easily appear as an ahistorical metaphysics with all the ready answers.[21] Indeed, it was for this very reason that Pope Leo XIII in his encyclical *Aeterni Patris* (1879) pushed the need for a Christian philosophy in accord with Aquinas in response to modernism — the legacy of which can easily be found in the form given to "philosophy of religion" textbooks that presuppose an abstract engagement with the arguments for the existence of God. Yet, as Healy points out, this proved entirely inadequate as a response, because rather than engaging with what was distinctive about theology (e.g., its doctrinal claims), it addressed modernity in terms of a natural theology, arguing on grounds already established by secularism.[22]

Little wonder, then, that de Lubac ran afoul of Catholic traditionalism. (He was asked to stop teaching Jesuits and his books were removed from Jesuit libraries.) Not only did his advocacy of historicism sound like creeping secularism, but by choosing Aquinas as his object of study he seemed to be undermining the neo-scholastics' best intentions. Added to this was the charge that the traditionalist Thomists, rather than representing the church's best defense against secularism, were secretly promoting it, a case of what Žižek would call an *inherent transgression*.[23]

The parallel with Lacan is striking here. First, Lacan's return to Freud was not simply a return to the founding father of psychoanalysis — often left by the wayside of the developing science — but a renewal of

21. Nicholas Healy, *Thomas Aquinas: Theologian of the Christian Life* (Aldershot: Ashgate, 2003), pp. 12-14.

22. Healy, *Thomas Aquinas*, p. 15.

23. For this reason it is not insignificant that Richard Dawkins's *The God Delusion* is partially predicated upon the critique of Aquinas. Dawkins's atheism is very much a failure of theology, not so much to prove God, but to have created the conditions — a realm of "pure" nature — under which God is a priori absent and therefore unknowable, not even by natural desire. Dawkins, *The God Delusion* (London: Black Swan, 2007), pp. 100-103.

the received interpretation. Second, like de Lubac, Lacan engaged the father through a close reading of the original texts with attention to the way they had been translated and contextualized. Third, one should consider the prior reception of Freud by the ego psychologists, the dominant school of the IPA (International Psychoanalytical Association) during the 1950s and 1960s. Early interpreters such as Freud's daughter Anna, Harry Guntrip, and Heinz Hartmann all argued that the self was in origin a bundle of self-seeking drives (the id) that should be brought into conformity through the rationalizing principle of the ego. So, given Freud's enigmatic claim "Wo Es war, soll Ich warden" (lit. where it was, I shall become) (É, 347/417),[24] the tendency was to translate it thus: "Where the id was, there the ego shall be" (É, 347/417) or "the ego must dislodge the id" (SXI, 44). On this reading the aim of analysis was directed toward the ego stamping out natural desire. By contrast, Lacan adopts what is arguably a more medieval approach, promoting the paradoxical unity of the two, *"Here, in the field of the dream, you are at home"* (SXI, 44). Indeed, Lacan explicitly identifies his criticism of ego psychology with the loss of the scholastic principle: "The antinomy the scholastic tradition posited as principal is here [in ego psychology] taken to be resolved" (É, 675/798).

In ego psychology the ego is set over and against the id rather than being intimately related to it. What we discover then in Lacan's renewal is, like de Lubac, an attempt to go beyond the schematism of the id/ego or nature/grace dualism, to arrive at new ways of speaking adequately about the real of human experience. Lacan encapsulates this paradoxical experience in his neologism "extimacy" (SVII, 139), by which he refers to the experience of the real as "something strange to me, although it is at the heart of me" (SVII, 71), an "intimate exteriority" (SVII, 139). It is possible that Lacan was influenced by the French Jesuit Teilhard de Chardin's concept of *intériorite*[25] or Pascal's fragment 793 where the interiority of man is said to transcend the universe as a whole: "All bodies, the firmament, the stars, the earth and its kingdoms, are not equal to the

24. This is also taken by Žižek as the title of his series for Verso.

25. Lacan explicitly refers to a dialogue he had with Teilhard de Chardin in Lacan, "Introduction to the Names-of-the-Father Seminar," trans. Jeffrey Mehlman, *October* 40 (Spring 1987): 81-95, 91.

lowest mind; for mind knows all these and itself." But both owe something to Augustine's theology of the interior life where *intimum* and *summum* coincide; the distant God is a God who is most near, nearer to man than man is to himself.

Moreover, one should not overlook the role played by Michel de Certeau, one among the sixty individuals who took part in the decisive meeting Lacan summoned to found his École Freudienne in 1960.[26] It was Certeau's meetings with de Lubac at the Catholic University at Lyons that initially encouraged Certeau to join the Society of Jesus in 1950. Little wonder, then, that Lacan, finding himself exiled by the IPA, was prompted to quip: "I am not saying — but it is not out of the question — that the psychoanalytic community is a church. But without doubt, the question arises if we are dealing with the echo of a religious practice,"[27] his fate curiously mirroring de Lubac's.

One should confer then with Richard R. Glejzer, who argued in "Lacan with Scholasticism" that "Lacan has more in common with the cosmology of the scholastics than he does with the linguistics of Saussure or Jakobson."[28]

My argument should also contribute to Erin Labbie's extraordinary thesis on the relation between Lacan and medieval thought: "My main focus . . . is to address the question of Lacan's medievalism; one aspect to this is to respond to Kristeva's question and assertion, 'Lacan a Thomist?' The question of Thomism is always one of balance between reason and faith. This is precisely what is at stake in believing the unconscious exists."[29] Kristeva's initial discussion concerned love and narcissism.[30] She made the link between the two with reference to the "primary

26. Luce Giard, "Michel de Certeau's Biography, Petite Bibliographie en anglais, par Luce Giard"; http:/www.jesuits.com/histoire/certeau.htm (accessed August 17, 2007).

27. Sherry Turkle, "Tough Love: An Introduction to Francoise Dolto's *When Parents Separate*"; http://web.mit.edu/sturkle/www/dolto.html (accessed August 16, 2007).

28. Richard Glejzer, "Lacan with Scholasticism: Agencies of the Letter," *American Imago* 54, no. 2 (1997): 105-22, 106.

29. Erin Labbie, *Lacan's Medievalism* (Minneapolis: University of Minnesota Press, 2006), p. 4.

30. See J. Kristeva, "Ratio Diligendi, or the Triumph of One's Own: Natural Love and Love of Self," in Kristeva, *Tales of Love,* trans. Leon Roudiez (New York: Columbia University Press, 1987), pp. 170-88.

message of Thomas Aquinas: love the other as oneself."[31] Her argument is that inner wounds have to be effectively healed before social intervention can take place: "we must heal our shattered narcissism before formulating higher objectives."[32] Kristeva is clearly at odds with Lacan, nonetheless, as Labbie explains, for belief in the unconscious requires both faith and reason for Lacan, and so his inquiry into the unconscious shares something of Aquinas's inquiry into God. In short, Lacan substitutes the God of Christian faith with the unconscious:

> As Christ was proof of God's existence, desire is proof of the existence of the unconscious. Both rely on a belief in the potential for the literal in language even while the recognition of that impossibility disrupts clear understanding. . . . As a limit case, God represents the aporia in logical and rational comprehension and points to the necessity of faith; as the limit case in the understanding of the human subject, the unconscious, represented by desire, calls for faith in the potential for unreason to untie the knot of language.[33]

According to Labbie, Lacan's theological reworking of the unconscious was made possible by the early influence of Jean Baruzi and Étienne Gilson. Baruzi was Lacan's teacher (1917-1918) and a rationalist Catholic thinker whom Roudinesco describes as bringing about a "transition of Lacan's thinking."[34] In place of the devout Catholicism practiced by his family, Lacan discovered a "scholarly, aristocratic Catholicism, one that might serve as a cultural substratum or critical instrument in the examination of things religious."[35] Central, too, was the part played by Étienne Gilson, the French medievalist who transformed Thomism and medieval studies in general for a generation of French intellectuals including

31. Kristeva, quoted in Kathleen O'Grady, "An Interview with Julia Kristeva," *Parallax: Julia Kristeva 1966-96. Aesthetics, Politics, Ethics* 8 (1998): 5-16, 8-11; http://www.cddc.vt.edu/feminism/Kristeva.html (accessed August 22, 2007).

32. Kristeva, quoted in O'Grady, "An Interview with Julia Kristeva."

33. Labbie, *Lacan's Medievalism*, p. 17.

34. Elisabeth Roudinesco, *Jacques Lacan*, trans. Barbara Bray (London: Polity, 1999), p. 12.

35. Roudinesco, *Jacques Lacan*, p. 12.

Baruzi and de Lubac. How then might Lacan qualify as a Thomist if not on the issue of love? Lacan "articulate[s] a form of 'Thomistic enquiry'"[36] on absent causality, i.e., on how the world was created ex nihilo. Lacan restages the question from the perspective of the desiring subject. How does the desiring subject emerge from *das Ding*, the constitutive void around which being coalesces (SVII, 67)?[37] Indeed, as Žižek points out, in place of the "symptom" (i.e., that which synthesizes — holds together — the subject's Universe) Lacan would sometimes use the neologism ÎLE SAINT HOMME, which itself recalls the name Saint Thomas (OB, 20).[38]

What, then, is the political upshot of this? First, as Milbank points out, once humanity accepts the realm of "pure nature," the very idea of teleology ceases to hold weight and creatureliness begins to be thought of, not in terms of its "normative maximum flourishing," i.e., its imaginative potentiality, but in terms of a "minimum self-sustainability."[39] When applied to humanity as a whole, this new creatureliness allows for the liberal conception of the individual and society, one "governed by the logic of preservation of material well-being and freedom."[40] Indeed, this was the exact model applied by Hobbes, the father of liberalism: humans, left to a state of nature, were self-seeking individuals whose sole motivation was the preservation of their own sphere of interest; therefore, it was in their best interest to enter a mutual contract, curbing some of their rights to secure their own private sphere of influence.

This easily translates into ego psychology in which the drives are taken as the primary expression of nature, a chaos that needs to be brought into social conformity through the rationalizing principle of the ego: *the ego must stamp out the id.* And like Hobbes, man would pass from nature to society through a contractual agreement; only now the con-

---

36. Labbie, *Lacan's Medievalism*, p. 18.

37. Labbie, *Lacan's Medievalism*, p. 18.

38. I suggest that the medieval underpinnings to Lacan's work go some way to suggesting why it took a medievalist, Sarah Kay, to write not only the first, but arguably the best, critical introduction to Žižek. See Kay, *Žižek: A Critical Introduction* (Cambridge: Polity, 2003).

39. John Milbank, *The Suspended Middle: Henri de Lubac and the Debate concerning the Supernatural* (Grand Rapids and Cambridge: Eerdmans, 2005), p. 21.

40. Milbank, *The Suspended Middle*, p. 21.

tractual agreement specifically targets the sexual relation: the ban upon incest. Yet it was precisely this model that Lacan was attacking, and at the same time as the French Jesuits and Dominicans were engaging in the critique of neo-scholasticism. It is possible then to draw out the deep historical ties that filter down, bringing together theology and psychoanalysis in the critique of liberalism and its political economy.

The influence of the theological debates on Žižek can be readily felt in the title of his Marxist defense of Christianity, *The Fragile Absolute*. The Absolute is not to be taken in the terms of onto-theology and metaphysics, i.e., as an extrinsic God, all-powerful and all-knowing, who dispenses grace to us down here on the earth; rather, God's grace is discerned through that most fragile of media, our earthly and bodily enjoyment.

Žižek's problem, however, arises because, despite the theological influence, he remains implicitly wedded to the neo-scholastic framework, giving credence to a supposed realm of "pure nature," *because only an extrinsic theology of grace could sustain a theology of tragic abandonment.* In other words, tragic abandonment makes sense only when the world is already presupposed to exist in absolute distinction from any supernatural appendage.

Perhaps drawing on the distinction initially introduced by Johannes Tauler, the fourteenth-century German mystic, one could call Žižek's abandonment a *false* abandonment, as opposed to a *true* abandonment: "In true abandonment everything is directed towards the supreme activity of worship. . . . False abandonment is prayer-less, whereas God wants to be prayed to. . . . While true abandonment is directed at an infinite liquidity of the heart, false abandonment leads to a petrification of the heart. . . . True abandonment means constantly giving back to God all He has given us and 'returning it all to the ground and source whence it sprang.'"[41]

A Dire-lectic

Žižek's theology of abandonment is clearly indebted to the mystical but ultimately heretical dialectic of Böhme, Schelling, Hegel, and Kierke-

41. Hans Urs von Balthasar, *The Glory of the Lord,* vol. 5, *The Realm of Metaphysics in the Modern Age* (Edinburgh: T. & T. Clark, 1991), pp. 53-54.

gaard. What all these writers share is a deeply Protestant theology of sin and grace, not unlike that found in the early Karl Barth. This can be identified in terms of the *overtly oppositional* logic of the terms. In the case of Barth, culture is so steeped in sin and the absolute brokenness of the world that any sense of hope can arrive only through a complete overturning of the world: grace. Such a viewpoint sits well with a theology of pure nature by presupposing the gulf between nature and grace. Yet a recovery of the medieval viewpoint suggests an alternative, albeit oppositional, logic, a *weak* dialectic, such that one pole is not required to *overcome* or, in Žižek's case, obliterate the other precisely because divine presence inhabits and permeates all material nature, rendering nature in its entirety as a holy sacrament. On this view, each dialectical pole remains to an extent a continual component of the other such that they perform a mutually critical correction of each other; a more relational as opposed to oppositional dialectic. This is not to give license back to a crude Augustinian view of sin by assuming its ontological priority; sin generates self-criticism but also the historical means for its outworking in the very formation of church.

Yet church is precisely the thing missing in Žižek's work. Consider Paul Griffiths's argument: "for Žižek the community brought into being by the Holy Spirit is not the Church. The Church could become the (true) Church, in his view, only if it, too, made the self-referential gesture of abnegation":[42] "In what is perhaps the highest example of Hegelian *Aufhebung*, it is possible today to redeem this core of Christianity only in the gesture of abandoning the shell of its institutional organization. . . . The gap here is irreducible: either one drops the religious form, or one maintains the form but loses the essence."[43] What Žižek does not see, according to Griffiths, is

that the Church here below is constituted precisely by the endless repetition of the self-abnegatory gestures he praises: the Pope is *servus servorum Dei* (the servant of the servants of God), the most powerful

42. Paul J. Griffiths, "Christ and Critical Theory," *First Things*, August/September 2004; http://www.firstthings.com/article.php3?id_article=372 (accessed October 10, 2007).

43. Žižek, quoted in Griffiths, "Christ and Critical Theory."

man in the world precisely because of his renunciation of power; the endlessly repeated eucharistic feast places the Church daily under erasure before its Lord; and the most characteristically ecclesial confession is that offered by Paul in 1 Timothy 1:15, according to which Paul is, he says, the first among sinners. Žižek may mean that no institutional form is appropriate to Christianity; but that would be a perfectionism which every good materialist (and Žižek claims to be one) should reject. If then there is an institutional form appropriate to the community brought into being by the Holy Spirit, Žižek offers no convincing reasons for denying that it is the Church.[44]

Ultimately, Žižek's rejection of church leads him away from the Catholicism of Lacan toward Protestant abandonism, which in turn commits him to a Gnostic rejection of the material by a refusal of the historical locality of the church.

Žižek and Derrida: Contrasting Negative Theologies

Matthew Sharpe is correct when he says Žižek finds himself in an "odd parity with the Derridean 'deconstructionism' he elsewhere stridently dismisses [because it] allows one to remain permanently dissident without being able to conceptualise the possibility of anything genuinely politically *redemptive* at all."[45] What then is the precise difference between Derrida's so-called negative theology and Žižek's theology of abandonment? Derrida himself recognized the similarities and distinctions between deconstruction and negative theology in a later essay: "From the moment a proposition takes a negative form, the negativity that manifests itself need only be pushed to the limit, and it at least resembles an apophatic theology."[46] In other words, "Just as 'sign' must be crossed out in the deconstructions of metaphysics, so too must 'God' in the decons-

44. Griffiths, "Christ and Critical Theory."

45. Matthew Sharpe, *Slavoj Žižek: A Little Piece of the Real* (Aldershot: Ashgate, 2004), p. 16.

46. Derrida, "How to Avoid Speaking: Denials," in *Derrida and Negative Theology,* ed. H. Coward and T. Foshay (Albany: SUNY Press, 1992), pp. 73-142, 76.

truction of positive theology."[47] But Derrida objected in vain to the assimilation of *différance* to negative theology. What distinguishes them is that negative theology nonetheless posits some "hyperessentiality: a being beyond Being."[48] That is to say, negative theologians still wager on onto-theological comprehension.

Here Žižek and Derrida are on common ground. Both pursue the *via negativa*, in thinking of a relation to that which exceeds our concepts (what Lacan calls the *real*), and end up with theologies that nonetheless refuse onto-theology. And both, like Meister Eckhart (the negative theologian who famously prayed to God to be rid of God), dramatize the failure of language, filling their work with paradox, contradiction, hyperbole, and negative images. In his recent work, however, Žižek has argued:

> Derrida emphasised that, the more radical a deconstruction is, the more it has to rely on its inherent "undeconstructible" condition of deconstruction, the messianic promise of justice. This promise is the true Derridiean object of *belief,* and the ultimate ethical axiom of Derrida is that this belief is irreducible, "undeconstructible." Derrida can thus indulge in all kinds of paradoxes, claiming, amongst other things, in his reflections on prayer, not only that atheists do pray, but that today, it is perhaps *only atheists who truly pray.* Precisely by refusing to address God as a positive entity, they silently address the pure messianic Otherness.[49]

Quite simply, Žižek's contention is that Derrida is not radical enough: Derrida throws away "all positive ontological content of messianism, retaining nothing but the pure form of the messianic promise,"[50] but

47. Kevin Hart, *The Trespass of the Sign: Deconstruction, Theology, and Philosophy* (Cambridge: Cambridge University Press, 1989), p. 202.

48. Derrida, "How to Avoid Speaking," p. 77.

49. Žižek, "A Plea for a Return to *Différance* (with a Minor *Pro Domo Sua*)," *Critical Inquiry* 32 (2006): 226-49, 231. Derrida's account of the "undeconstructible" kernel of deconstruction can be found in Derrida, *Acts of Religion,* trans. S. Weber, ed. Gil Anidjar (New York: Routledge, 2001), p. 243.

50. Žižek, "A Plea," p. 232.

Derrida does not go far enough; he does not throw away the form itself.[51] Žižek himself describes the difference in terms of the passage from Judaism to Christianity. "Judaism reduces the promise of another life to a pure Otherness, a messianic promise that will never become fully present and actualised (the Messiah is always 'to come'), while Christianity, far from claiming full realisation of the promise, accomplishes something far more uncanny: the Messiah is *here,* he *has* arrived, the final Event already took place, *and yet the gap (the gap that sustained the messianic promise) remains.*"[52]

One way to describe the difference between the theologies of Derrida and Žižek is in terms of the diachronic and the synchronic. Derrida's theology locates the messianic promise in the as-yet-to-come, i.e., within time, albeit not-as-yet, permanently promised, while Žižek's theology of abandonment concerns a structural, and constitutive, ontological gap. Indeed, this is precisely the issue at stake in Žižek's recent critique of Derrida: "What if the idea of infinite messianic justice that operates in an indefinite suspension, always to come, as the 'undeconstructible' horizon of deconstruction, already obfuscates the 'pure' *différance,* the pure gap that differs an entity from itself."[53]

Another way to map their differences is by way of the theological distinction between the cataphatic and the apophatic, the latter being traditionally associated with the *via negativa.*[54] The former formulates true statements about God, either through reason *(theosophia)* or divine revelation *(theologia);* the latter demonstrates their incomprehensibility. Derrida's work tends toward the apophatic, ensuring against too narrow, literal, or idolatrous a claim; Žižek's work tends toward the cataphatic: the point is to recognize that the Messiah is *here,* he *has* arrived.

Yet Žižek's theology of abandonment makes sense only if the point *is* to recognize that the Messiah has arrived and hence politics *can* be, as Matthew Sharpe says, "redemptive"; it makes sense if God *is* known in creation while paradoxically distinct, i.e., "extimate" (SVII, 139), because

51. Žižek, "A Plea," p. 232.
52. Žižek, "A Plea," pp. 232-33.
53. Žižek, "A Plea," p. 233.
54. Bruce Milem, "Four Theories of Negative Theology," *Heythrop Journal* 48 (2007): 187-204.

otherwise it slips into the same formalism by which he criticizes Derrida. In other words, if we do not read it as theology proper, we are left with the form of the Event that is, in regard to the Left, as-yet-to-come. That is to say, Žižek makes sense if we read him not as he reads Derrida; i.e., Žižek employs Christianity as an example by which we may establish a change. Nonetheless, it is not actually Christianity that matters, but its form (abnegation) that gives a clue to the means of revolution; rather one should read Žižek in the mode *of* Žižek, i.e., it is time for the Left to take theology not simply for its examples and models, but absolutely seriously if the Left is to make sense of itself.

Liberal Multiculturalism versus Christian Incarnation

According to Žižek, the Left has abdicated its responsibility to an economic critique, choosing instead to focus on identity politics, taking up the causes of various minority groups while promoting more generally an ethical awareness of the "other," a respect for multiculturalism in a global era. And nowhere is this more evident than in the popularity of "cultural studies," of which Žižek is arguably a victim. By this I mean that he is not read theologically, and hence theology is held at bay by the cultural theorists. Foucault, Derrida, and Said have all joined the charge against grand narratives and universal theories, each highlighting in his particular way the various means by which an espoused universal assumption (e.g., freedom and democracy) really masks the interests of a particular group (i.e., Western liberals).

Žižek is highly critical of liberal multiculturalism and "the standard multiculturalist's idea that, against ethnic intolerance, one should learn to respect and live with the Otherness of the Other" (FA, 11); otherness is not the ethical horizon. His reasons are four. First, multiculturalism misrepresents the task of the Left. The Left need not concern itself with ensuring respect for local customs and minority groups against the hegemony of global capitalism. After all, local customs already thrive, often side by side, within our global cities. Rather, what should be of concern is the very model of economic globalism itself. As Žižek says: "I don't accept as the level of a modern left the so-called identitarian struggles of postmodern multiculturalism: gay rights, ethnic minority demands, tolerance politics, anti-patriarchal movements and so on. I am more and more convinced that these are upper-middle-class phenomena which shouldn't be accepted as the horizon of struggle for the left. To avoid any misunderstanding, I am not opposed to multi-culturalism as such; what I am opposed to is the idea that it constitutes the fundamental struggle of today" (C, 144).

Second, an ethics of tolerance and respect is "fake and patronising" (C, 123) because respect is merely formal, empty, or nonsubstantive. Žižek's argument is quite simple: when the moral position par excellence becomes one of not judging — i.e., *you can do what you want as long as it doesn't affect me* — morality has turned into its inverse; because to take someone seriously is to be critical, to consider that person worthy of critical engagement. As Žižek points out, should one simply learn to respect the Hindu custom of burning wives? In other words, we need to be able to generate critical dialogue that also implies a certain risk on the part of all those concerned: in trying to change the other's mind in determining what is best for the polity, one also risks having one's own mind changed.

Third, although taken as an expression of political freedom, multiculturalism exercises a perverse subjection because we never accept the other *as such*. As Žižek says: "We in the West — we Western liberals that is — already presume the authority of neutral judgement, but we do not accept the other as such. We implicitly introduce a certain limit. We test the Other against our notions of human rights, dignity and equality of sexes and then, to put it in slightly cynical terms, we say we accept those of your customs which pass this test. We already filter the Other. . . . What we get at the end is a censored Other" (C, 124).

Žižek's fourth point is a little more subtle and requires some unpacking. It starts as a variant of Nietzsche's problematic: one cannot make the claim that *all truth is relative* (i.e., the product of a particular historical interest) without subsequently turning relativity into the new absolute, or as Maurice Blondel put it in 1893: "one cannot exclude metaphysics except by a metaphysical critique."[55] By transposing this to cultural studies,

---

55. Maurice Blondel, *Action: Essay on a Critique of Life and a Science of Practice*, trans. Oliva Blanchette (Notre Dame, Ind.: University of Notre Dame Press, 1984), p. 358.

Žižek makes the point that the general theoretical framework of cultural studies fails to take into account that historicism is also historical.[56] He presents his argument thus: "The truly radical assertion of historical contingency has to include the dialectical tension between the domain of historical change itself and its traumatic 'ahistorical' kernel *qua* its condition" (CHU, 211-12). What is at stake here is the way the current vogue for historicizing all claims — what Žižek calls *historicism* — quickly turns into a new form of ideology that totalizes the field, paradoxically, undermining the possibility of *historicity proper.*

Everything hangs on this distinction: *historicism* and *historicity proper. Historicism* deals with the "endless play of substitutions [differing forms of historical criticism/deconstruction] within the same fundamental field" (CHU, 112). The historicist theme thereby becomes "the very form of ahistorical ideological closure" (CHU, 112). By contrast, *historicity proper* is able to bring the very field of reference itself into question, reconfigure the very sets of relations that allow thought to think the way it does. Historicity proper therefore includes the possibility of *actual* change at the level of the paradigm itself, and therefore makes the shift from cultural studies to radical politics.

The difference here is analogous to the difference introduced by Kierkegaard between recollection and repetition.[57] The doctrine of recollection, a pagan category, attends to the Sophistic dilemma concerning knowledge: "One can never find out anything new: either one knows it already, in which case there is no need to find it, or else one does not and in that case there is no means of recognising it when found."[58] The doctrine of recollection holds that the soul is immortal, and in the course of its transmigration through the cosmos has learned everything;

56. In an interview with *Radical Philosophy,* Žižek explains that in the Republics of Yugoslavia — Slovenia, Croatia, Serbia — different theoretical traditions predominated. In Slovenia the conflict was between Western Marxists (the Left) and dissident Heideggerians (the Right). Critical theory, underpinning cultural studies, was viewed as a political alternative by the new Slovenian philosophers. Thus Žižek's disillusionment with cultural studies is a disillusionment with the aspiring liberal critique of Slovenian politics that he himself was a part of; see Žižek, "Lacan in Slovenia," p. 25.

57. Kierkegaard, *Repetition/Fear and Trembling,* trans. H. Hong and E. Hong (Princeton: Princeton University Press, 1983), p. 131.

58. Plato, *Meno,* trans. W. K. C. Guthrie (Middlesex: Penguin Books, 1981), p. 104, E.80.

all knowledge is therefore situated latent in the mind. Learning is a matter of *recollecting* or remembering what is latent, and this latent content forms the basis of self-knowledge. How does this accord with historicism? Just as historicism fails to question the historicist paradigm as a whole, so too for Plato, any new piece of self-knowledge gained cannot bring the self as a whole into question, because the self is already presupposed to have known it. Learning is only ever finding out what we already knew, and hence lacks the possibility of introducing a decisive *change* in the subject. Such a viewpoint follows the *novissima prima:* the unchanging principle.

Repetition, by contrast, is a Christian category, the highest expression of which is atonement. In repetition one receives oneself back *anew,* passing from the position of untruth (i.e., sin) to truth (conversion). Repetition therefore implies a sense of continuity — like the doctrine of recollection — but also a dramatic sense of change, because it introduces something new that transcends the conditions that determine it: revelation. It cannot be the case that one realizes what was already implicit within one because genuine change implies that one becomes *other* than what one was, and according to Kierkegaard, this cannot be done on one's own merit, but only through God: God gives us ourselves back. So whereas recollection is circumscribed by immanence (one recollects what one already knew), repetition involves transcendence. How does repetition relate to historicity proper: because repetition includes the possibility of *actual* change, of becoming something new, rather than discovering what was already known? Repetition, like historicity proper, is therefore on the side of radical politics.

The question remains: How does one make the shift from the immanent historicism of cultural studies (i.e., relativism) to historicity proper (i.e., radical politics)? The answer: by recourse to some "traumatic 'ahistorical' kernel qua [the] condition of (im)possibility" (CHU, 112). Žižek's point is that only when history is grounded in universality does historicity proper arise. But what exactly is the status of the universal? The universal is identified with the *real.* This is not the traditional way of conceptualizing a universal; it is not a description in the order of positivity, a genus such as the universal "man" under which species may be gathered. Rather, the universal is found in the *real* of experience, the exception that gives rise to the whole. As Žižek explains, "The universal (in its difference to the empirical generality) is constituted through the exception; we do not pass from the general set to the universal of One-Notion by way of adding something to the set but, on the contrary, by way of subtracting something from it, namely the 'unitary feature' which totalises the general set" (FTKN, 123).

To clarify the above, we can again refer to Kierkegaard's argument against the Greeks and the pagans. In *The Concept of Anxiety* (1844) Kierkegaard points to two differing approaches to time that broadly correspond to his distinction between recollection and repetition: the Greek/pagan approach to time and a specifically Christian approach to time.[59] According to Kierkegaard, the pagans conflate eternity and time: eternity is simply time as it stretches infinitely backward or forward along the chain of succession that passes. By contrast the Christian claim is that the Eternal *enters* time (i.e., the incarnation), although it is not reducible to time. This was the point of the early formulation of Christ's identity at the Chalcedon Council in 451: Christ is neither two separate persons — if he were, his divinity would remain distinct from his temporal nature — nor are those two elements resolved into a single nature. Rather, Christ is one person whose divine (eternal) nature is the exception that grounds his humanity (temporality). In short, one can identify directly this traumatic element of the Eternal, i.e., divinity, with what Žižek calls the universal.

But how exactly does this difference account for the dramatic shift from historicism to historicity proper? Why should recourse to some traumatic "ahistorical" kernel be constitutive of time (CHU, 112)? Because, confronted by the traumatic real (i.e., the universal), time cannot but matter in new ways.

This was Heidegger's point: an encounter with our mortal temporality makes us sensitive to history. From the encounter stems awareness that we are rooted in the past and thrust into the future. For Heidegger, then, time is not simply a series of "now's,"[60] part of a great chain that

59. Kierkegaard, *The Concept of Anxiety,* trans. R. Thomte (Princeton: Princeton University Press, 1980), pp. 85-91.

60. Heidegger, *Being and Time,* trans. J. Macquarrie and E. Robinson (Oxford: Blackwell, 1983), p. 474.

trails back into the forgotten past while stretching forward into the great unknown. Rather, time is an existential category in which the past and future meet in the possibilities and decisions we embrace in the present. The past refers to the way we are already in the world, the way prior events or tradition has shaped, determined, or opened up possibilities for us. But our past also gets meaning from our future[61] because it is re-defined as new events retroactively cast light on what went before. The future illuminates the past in different ways that can coterminously af-fect the present anew, so the actuality of what has been depends upon the possibilities of what we do with it.

The existential standpoint proves decisive for Christianity as power-fully conveyed through the eucharistic doctrine of anamnesis. In anamnesis one remembers the past, not as a fact that figured within a causal chain of events, but as a promise given in the past, which deter-mines the Christian community in the present. The present is not self-sufficient with regard to the past, but takes its meaning from the past promise, which comes back in the form of eschatological hope from the future.[62]

And this approach also proves decisive for Žižek because it is only by recourse to the real of experience that temporality is manifested in such a way as to allow for historicity proper, i.e., radical politics. Žižek calls it the universal; Kierkegaard calls it the incarnation: "Kierkegaard was right when he pointed out the central opposition in Western spirituality is between Socrates and Christ: the inner journey of remembrance versus rebirth through the shock of the external encounter. Within the Jewish-Christian field, God Himself is the ultimate harasser, the intruder who brutally disturbs the harmony of our lives" (L, 99).

What is the status of this relation: the universal and incarnation? If we accept Žižek's argument, that Christianity took the eternal as distinct from time in contrast to the Greeks, then it would appear to confirm Milbank's argument: "The universality of Christianity is not therefore a matter of subjective opinion or of faith in the first place; it is rather a

---

61. "The character of 'having been' arises, in a certain way, from the future." Heidegger, *Being and Time*, p. 373.

62. *Catechism of the Catholic Church*, §1354.

matter of logic. Christianity is universal because it invented the logic of universality; it constituted this logic as an event."[63]

It appears, then, that there is a third way, between the Scylla of cultural studies and the Charybdis of cultural imperialism: the realm of historicity and radical politics proper, i.e., theology. But it cannot be the neo-pagan variant offered up by Žižek. Žižek simply conjures up Christ as the "ultimate sublime object," with the offer to reconcile us to the void.[64] In doing so, he offers but a variant of Derrida's "religion without religion":[65] a kind of rootless religiosity and stammering apophasis with no attention to the cataphatic. Žižek's Christian, in the terms of Milbank, is a nomadic wanderer, stripped of any final positive ontological goal, and hence, while his theory is able to sustain an ontology of revolution, there is little chance of socialism.[66]

63. Milbank, "Materialism and Transcendence," p. 401.
64. Milbank, "Materialism and Transcendence," p. 398.
65. Derrida, "How to Avoid Speaking," pp. 73-142.
66. Milbank, "Materialism and Transcendence," p. 404.

CHAPTER 4

Sexual Difference and Non-All *(Pas-tout)*

In *The Knowledge of the Analyst,* Lacan recounts how, prior to the publication of *The Second Sex* (1949), Simone de Beauvoir called him on the telephone to clarify what should be the psychoanalytic contribution to her work. Lacan said it would take him at least five to six months to disentangle the question, to which de Beauvoir replied that "there was no question, of course, that a book that was already in train should wait so long, the laws of literary production being such." At best she could afford three or four conversations. Lacan declined the honor but not the question, although it would take another twenty years before he began to formulate his thought, culminating in his *formulae of sexuation* and accompanying claim: "there is no second sex from the moment that language comes into function."[1] In his engagement with Lacan, Žižek has done much to clarify Lacan's obtuse work on gender and sexuality.[2] However, his work on gender is also marked by a deep religious engagement to the extent that Lacan's debates on sexuality provide the key to understanding the place of Christianity within Žižek's thought. The aim of this chapter is to critically explore that relation.

---

1. Lacan, "The Knowledge of the Analyst" (1971-1972), trans. Cormac Gallagher (unpublished manuscript), session V, March 3, 1972, p. 4.

2. Žižek, "Concesso non Dato," in *Traversing the Fantasy: Critical Responses to Slavoj Žižek,* ed. G. Boucher, J. Glynos, and M. Sharpe (Aldershot: Ashgate, 2005), pp. 219-56, 239.

ŽIŽEK

The Formulae of Sexuation

It may strike the reader as strange that in attending to the question of sexual difference Lacan directly employed Frege's formal logic. Is this not typical of a man to describe sexuality and gender in cold, disembodied, and rational terms? However, one does well to recall that, first, what is at stake is an account of gender, not simply anatomical factors, but the psychical differences between masculinity and femininity. These differences are not simply instinctual or natural, but arise from the complex interaction of social-psychological factors. In short, the sexed body is already overwritten by signifiers. Second, the context in which Lacan was writing was second wave feminism. In contrast to first wave feminism (i.e., women should be equal to men, although masculinity remains the norm), second wave feminists tried to claim the existence of a specifically feminine universal. To be equal was for women to claim their own rights qua the feminine. The problem arose for second wave feminism because it took as normative the concept of an eternal mother. This was the image through which women could recognize their own true nature. The problem, then, as Lacan understood it, was that this easily lapsed back into an essentialist discourse about women in which all women were identified primarily as mothers. The implications for psychoanalytic practice could not be more problematic: analysts tended to presuppose what a woman was (i.e., a mother), and this allowed the analyst to frame in advance her problem without taking into account the specificity of each woman in the clinical setting.

The use of the formulae therefore tackled head-on the essentialism of second wave feminism. What they offer is not a list of essentialist predicates to describe in positive terms the distinctions between men and women (for example, men are aggressors, women are protectors, etc.), but two distinct descriptions of the antagonisms one encounters precisely when one tries to determine what masculinity and femininity are. As Lacan says: "The sexual relationship . . . can no longer be written in terms of male essence and female essence."[3] Lacan's formulae are as follows:

3. Lacan, "Knowledge of the Analyst," session V, March 3, 1972, p. 10.

Sexual Difference and Non-All (Pas-tout)

Masculine		Feminine	
$\exists X$	$\overline{\Phi X}$	$\overline{\exists X}$	$\overline{\Phi X}$
$\forall X$	ΦX	$\overline{\forall X}$	ΦX

Fig. 1. Seminar XX, p. 78.

The formulae employ recognizable logical propositions: *quantifiers*. The backward *E* is the *existential* quantifier; it refers to a *particular X*. Placed in the left-hand box, *X* refers to the masculine subject; placed in the right-hand box, *X* refers to the feminine subject. The upside-down *A* is the *universal* quantifier; hence it refers to *all Xs* (either all men or all women). The formulae also include an original proposition: Φ stands for phallic *jouissance*, i.e., pleasure or enjoyment. A horizontal line placed above the formulae negates the proposition. To read the formulae, one begins with either side and reads it vertically in terms of the antagonism or logical contradiction that exists *between* the two propositions that belong on that side. The logical contradiction that arises within each set gives expression to the fundamental antagonism by which Lacan identifies either the masculine or the feminine subject. Hence gender is not a matter of biology, but a structural position.

Masculine	**Feminine**
There exists an *x* (i.e., a man) who is *not* subject to phallic *jouissance*.	There is not one *x* (i.e., female) who is not subject to phallic *jouissance*.
All *x* (i.e., men) are subject to phallic *jouissance*.	not-All *x* (i.e., women) are subject to phallic *jouissance*.

105

Masculinity

The antagonism that defines masculinity is readily common. It can be read as the law of exception; i.e., for every rule there is an exception that paradoxically grounds the rule. The most salient example of this is in *Totem and Taboo,* where Freud developed Darwin's myth of the primal father. According to Freud, men lived in relatively small groups within which the strongest male jealously prevented sexual promiscuity by keeping all the females for himself. Hence, while all men were subject to his phallic law, there existed one male who was not, yet nonetheless by which the law itself was grounded (SE, 13:125). On the basis of this example, one can also describe the masculine formula of sexuation in terms of castration: all men are castrated, but there is one exception that proves the rule. The exception has the function of the father who subsequently establishes the set of men, thereby allowing for a unitary trait: all men are castrated.

Femininity

The antagonism that defines femininity is described as the *not-All (pas-tout).* The upper line in the above figure states that there is not one particular woman who is not subject to phallic *jouissance.* In other words, all women fall under the rule of the phallus. This controversial claim is easily discernible in the Romance languages such as French or Italian where regardless of one's anatomical sex, one must use a language that takes as its normative the masculine. For example, in Italian, given a group of ten babies where nine are female and one is male, the plural always takes the masculine form: *bambini;* hence all women are subject to phallic law.

The lower line reads: "not-All *x* (i.e., women) are subject to phallic *jouissance.*" "Not-all" does not mean *not-at-all,* i.e., that women are entirely outside the symbolic or patriarchal rule. Nor is it meant to imply *all-not-phallic,* i.e., that there is a universal and integral essence of woman as distinct from an essence of masculinity, grounding women as a set. Rather, to say that woman is not-All is to say precisely that there is no single exception that allows for a universal set of women to emerge, or there is no unitary trait that functions for women in the way castration does for men: there are only particulars, and hence *each* woman *is* an exception. In short, woman is only ever singular and henceforth the very principle of difference. For this reason Lacan would write, "~~The~~ woman does not exist," crossing out the article to underscore the point: there is no objectifying or unifying article for woman. This is an important point. In the early translations of Lacan's text, it was "woman" that was crossed out, as if to say there is no such thing as woman; Lacan's point is that there is no objectifying trait that defines woman as a whole in the way that castration defines men as a whole.

The Return to Freud

To clarify Lacan's distinction, one should return to Freud's thought concerning the acquisition of masculine and feminine sexuality. According to Freud, masculinity could be easily accounted for in terms of the Oedipus complex: the boy's love for the mother is triangulated by the castration complex, by which he abandons sexual love for the mother and internalizes the beloved father (i.e., the logic of exception). In this way the child becomes subject to law. However, whereas men could quite readily identify with the father simply by virtue of anatomy, the journey for women involved changing the love object, i.e., abandoning sexual love for the mother to identify with the opposite sex. For this reason Freud would go on to say that whereas the castration complex resolves the Oedipus complex for boys, it spells the start of a process for girls, a process for which there is no clear resolution (SE, 16:332-37). In other words, there is no clear symbol of feminine sexuality to guide the girl. Little wonder that Freud would later refer to woman as "a dark continent" (SE, 20:212).

The problematic nature of feminine sexuality was further complicated for Freud by the normative role given the phallus. Freud observed that when the little boy sees the girl's genitals, he denies the lack of penis but sees something small that will grow bigger. He reasoned that for girls the perceived lack of a penis gives rise to penis envy, the desire for a penis, a desire only resolved in part by giving birth to a male child.

Freud floundered in his attempt to account for feminine sexuality, i.e., to identify a single unitary trait. By contrast, as Elizabeth O'Loughlin argues, it was precisely in this impasse that Lacan saw the importance of Freud's discovery: feminine sexuality arises precisely because she cannot be accounted for in Oedipal terms.[4] In other words, where Freud encountered an impasse, he still believed that one day psychoanalysts would be able to account for feminine sexuality in positive terms. By contrast, Lacan made the impasse the very point. This is the Freudian meaning of Lacan's claim "The woman does not exist"; it attests to the fact that there is no symbol of the feminine sex in the unconscious. This is not to deny the anatomical reality of girls; it means simply that "feminine sex cannot be raised to the status of the signifier. . . . It is foreclosed from the structure."[5] Femininity therefore represents a limit to the unconscious. The unconscious is not simply a buried container, full of repressed images that could in theory be recovered. Rather, there is something unrepresentable even in the unconscious: feminine sexuality. It is not that femininity is repressed; it is that it doesn't exist as a unitary trait and so exposes the lack in masculinity. This is why Lacan subtitled his seminar on femininity "The Limits of Love and Knowledge."

At this point it would be easy to contest Žižek's work on the grounds that woman is predominantly defined in terms of lack. Yet as Claude-Noële Pickmann has argued, this need not be taken as negatively as one might suspect. For instance, in regard of woman, it implies a "great[er] freedom in the way of being referred to the phallic function" because not only are there as many ways as there are women, but also, for each woman, there are "as many ways as she will come across."[6] For this reason, Lacan referred to castration as "norm-male," i.e., as the norm for masculinity. Men are able to share a common identity as castrated, grounded in the exception. By contrast, women have no such unitary trait; theirs is the logic of the not-All.[7] Hence women should not be re-

4. Elizabeth O'Loughlin, "Why Can't a Woman Be More Like a Man?" (seminar paper, Sevenside, Bristol, November 11, 2006).

5. Claude-Noële Pickmann, "Examining a Clinic of the Not-All," *The Letter: Lacanian Perspectives on Psychoanalysis,* Spring 2004, pp. 19-30, 23.

6. Pickmann, "Examining a Clinic," p. 24.

7. Grace Jantzen misinterprets Lacan on this point. She thinks his claim that it is "the

duced to mothers, nor are women simply the "other set" to "men"; instead they may be considered the "open-set" (SXX, 9-10).

It was such an account of woman that led Lacan in Seminar XX to posit a *jouissance* specific to each woman. By this Lacan implied a *jouissance* not circumscribed by the order of castration, a *jouissance* given finest expression in Bellini's statue of the mystic Saint Theresa. Freud was blinded by a phallic cause; he made libido masculine and masculinity normative. Freud was therefore unable to envisage a register of woman that escaped masculinity, i.e., a specifically feminine *jouissance.* For Lacan, woman is not lacking in *jouissance* — after all, she is submitted fully within the field of phallic *jouissance* — but she also has a supplementary *jouissance,* beyond what she finds in the phallic field. This is not an "extra" *jouissance* in the sense of a pleasure that arises because woman has something *else* in addition to what men have; it is the qualitative experience of not being grounded in an exception, i.e., the *jouissance* of the pure material immanence of woman in her being.

Femininity *Is* Atheism

In her essay "Examining a Clinic of the Not-All," Claude-Noële Pickmann says the not-All constitutes a "particular treatment of the Ideal, albeit a dismissal. In this, one can say that the *not-all* is atheistic in itself."[8] Her comments point us in the direction of Žižek. Žižek reads the logic of the not-All as the critique of onto-theology or overcoming of metaphysics. Onto-theology relies on the structure of masculinity, the logic of an exception that proves the rule. In this case the father in question is God, the omnipotent and omniscient father who stands outside the system as a kind of transcendental placeholder, sustaining the system as a whole. In short, God is the exception that grounds the law. God cannot be reduced to the order of Being, because he defines the order and hence law;

---

sexual characteristics of the mother which predominate in woman" is a repetition of the "oldest and most banal of sexist stereotypes" rather than a genuine challenge. Grace Jantzen, *Becoming Divine: Towards a Feminist Philosophy of Religion* (Manchester: Manchester University Press, 1998), p. 41 n. 2.

8. Pickmann, "Examining a Clinic," p. 25.

nonetheless, by accepting castration, it is possible to internalize those predicates: man is omnipotent within the order of being. Femininity therefore proves challenging — one might even say *traumatic* — because it raises the specter that "there is no Other of the Other," i.e., there is no set of women guaranteed by a primal [m]Other. Hence femininity occupies the position of the atheist; women's is the cry of dereliction.

To underline this point, Žižek explicitly links the relation between the feminine logic of not-All and the masculine logic of the exception with the critique of ideology by way of theology:

> The situation is here homologous to the common notion of God as a person criticised by Spinoza: in their endeavour to understand the world around them . . . people sooner or later arrive at the point at which their understanding fails, encounter a limit, and God . . . merely gives body to this limit. . . . The first operation of the critique of ideology is therefore to recognise in the fascinating presence of God the filler of gaps in the structure of knowledge. . . . And our point is that it is somewhat homologous with the feminine "not-all": this not-all does not mean that woman is not entirely submitted to the Phallus; it rather signals that she sees through the fascinating presence of the Phallus, that she is able to discern in it the filler of the inconsistency of the Other.[9]

The challenge of femininity is the challenge of pure immanence, a point that the French sociologist Jean Baudrillard would reiterate some two years later in his controversial polemic *Seduction* (1979). Baudrillard points out that the feminist movement has traditionally been opposed to the characterization of women as artifice or surface, i.e., they are concerned only with appearances. Such characterizing, they argue, fails to recognize their "true being." However, Baudrillard points out that it is precisely by remaining at the level of appearance that women are able to thwart masculine depth. Women seduce through appearances, and appearances never accede to truth or meaning in the onto-theological

---

9. Žižek, "Woman Is One of the Names-of-the-Father," *Lacanian Ink* 10 (1995); http://www.lacan.com/zizwoman.htm (accessed July 16, 2007).

sense of the word.[10] This is a subtle point. Baudrillard is not saying that women are superficial in the pejorative sense — although he clearly plays on the emotional resonances of the term — but that femininity is postmetaphysical and that it is this status that proves so challenging to an order predicated upon metaphysics (i.e., onto-theology).

Žižek and Feminism

With regard to the specificity of Žižek's work, it might be argued that he does little to endear himself to the feminist cause. For example, he describes the antipatriarchal movements as "upper-middle-class phenomena which shouldn't be accepted as the horizon of struggle for the left" (C, 144). Moreover, it is not difficult to apply the standard feminist critique to his work: Žižek is unable to think of woman as other than lack, negativity, or incomplete, and while this may be descriptively true, by perpetuating it as a theoretical position it becomes prescriptive. As for language, it remains as it was for Lacan, a substitute for the body of the mother. And because the key to language lies in what Lacan called the symbolic phallus, masculinity becomes normative of culture: where women speak, they do so only by appropriating masculine language.[11] This is the criticism made by Claudia Breger, who adds that Žižek's "Christianised *feminine jouissance*"[12] has the effect of displacing political agency into the transcendental outer realms, insulated against contemporary action.

By Žižek's own standards, it might also be argued that his theory is of itself a figment of the male imaginary, i.e., a narcissistic means of shor-

10. Jean Baudrillard, *Seduction,* trans. Brian Singer (New York: St. Martin's Press, 1990), p. 8.

11. It is then no surprise that Britain's first female prime minister, Baroness Thatcher, greatly favored her tabloid nickname: *the Iron Lady.* This explains why Lacan favored logic to describe sexual difference because, as Claude-Noële Pickmann puts it, "what cannot be grasped through signification, since this is always phallic, can be surrounded by logic." Pickmann, "Examining a Clinic," p. 20.

12. Claudia Breger, "The Leader's Two Bodies: Slavo Žižek's Postmodern Political Theology," *Diacritics* 31, no. 1 (2001): 73-90, 86.

ing up male identity and masculinity as the dominant power base. For this reason, any move to equality is compromised from the start because women are always going to be deficient. Indeed, Žižek consistently situates women on the side of the *real* and masculinity on the side of the symbolic. This implies, as Freud implied before him, that culture is built upon the repression of women: the negation of woman, as the condition of the symbolic. In other words, woman is associated with a material existence, which needs to be extinguished. In this way woman is coupled with death; and hence when Žižek refers to her as plenitude, it is not in her capacity to bear life, the gift of the womb, but in her capacity as the unbearable *Thing*, the *nihilo* or *real* of experience that threatens to smother one should she become too close.[13]

In his defense, however, it can be argued, first, as Žižek has maintained, that "the focus of [his] detailed reading of Lacan's 'formulas of sexuation' is that, precisely, women are more included in the symbolic than men."[14] In other words, his aim is to do as much to clarify Lacan's thought on sexuality and gender as possible, with a view to engaging feminist thought.

Second, his criticism of the feminist movement is a critique not of feminism per se, but of the level at which it puts its argument. The problem arises when feminism is expressed in terms of identity politics, seeking inclusion within the existing symbolic rather than bringing the symbolic as a whole into question. This is the weakness of the Jungian approach, which thinks predominantly in terms of two different sexes (animus/anima) that nonetheless come together to form a complementary whole (what Jung called the *contra*-sexual couple). As Žižek explains, the moment one accepts this approach, one is lost. The problem arises because there is no way to provide a neutral account of the terms of the balance. In other words, the political task of feminism should not concern itself with the difference between masculine and feminine, with women asking for better representation because men and women will differ in the very way they see the difference between the sexes. It is in this sense that Žižek aims toward universality because what is at stake is not a posi-

13. This is Grace Jantzen's criticism of Lacan; see Jantzen, *Becoming Divine*, pp. 34-54.
14. Žižek, "Concesso non Dato," p. 239.

tion within a given frame, but the very frame itself. As Žižek says: "This is what you must be conscious of, that when you fight for your position, you at the same time fight for the universal frame of how your position will be perceived within this universal frame. This is for me, as every good feminist will tell you, the greatness of modern feminism. It's not just we women want more. It's we women want to redefine the very universality of what it means to be human. This is for me this modern notion of political struggle."[15] This is why defining femininity — like masculinity — is best undertaken through formal logic, which gives expression to a particular form of antagonism; because it resists reducing sexual identity to identity politics, i.e., defining masculinity and femininity in terms of an essence within the order of positivity, such that one might say, for example, *"woman is by nature . . ."* (IR, 335). For Žižek, to speak of an "essence" of "woman" is not to posit some positive entity; rather, it names the very deadlock that prevents her from becoming woman, i.e., singular. The presentation of the formulae opens the way for a denaturized subject, a subject without natural properties. In this way Žižek can be said to share the concerns of Luce Irigaray: by predetermining woman's role in advance, we risk paralyzing the "infinite becoming of woman."[16]

Third, as the impossibility of the sexual relation stems from the split within each subject, Žižek makes sexual difference not merely a struggle among others, but the very index of all struggles (OB, 43), again, a point by no means at odds with strands of feminism such as Luce Irigaray's.

Fourth, while Žižek does principally associate the feminine with the real, he nonetheless offers subtle subversions of the standard picture. A case in point is his essay "Otto Weininger, or 'Woman Doesn't Exist'" (ME, 137-66). Weininger made a name for himself with his polemical antifeminist work *Sex and Character* (1903), and although Žižek initially endorses Weininger's central thesis (women have no subjectivity of their own), he does so in such a way as to highlight Lacan's thesis: women's inconsistency is precisely what allows them to find a nonphallic enjoyment, i.e., an enjoyment not circumscribed by masculinity.

15. http://www.lacan.com/zizek-human.htm (accessed March 15, 2008).

16. Luce Irigaray, "Divine Women," in *French Feminists on Religion: A Reader*, ed. M. Joy et al. (London and New York: Routledge, 2002), p. 42.

Likewise, when Žižek says that "woman is a symptom of man," he is not reducing woman to a male fantasy. He is arguing that

> *man himself exists only through woman qua his symptom:* all his onto-logical consistency hangs on, is suspended from his symptom, is "externalized" in his symptom. In other words, man literally *ex-sists:* his entire being lies "out there," in woman. Woman, on the other hand, does *not* exist, she *insists,* which is why she does not come to be through man only — there is something in her that escapes the rela-tion to man, the reference to the phallic signifier; and, as is well known, Lacan attempted to capture this excess by the notion of a *"not-all" feminine jouissance.* (EYS, 155-56)

Jewish Masculinity versus Christian Feminism:
From Law to Love

In "The Real of Sexual Difference" Žižek claims it is by way of the passage from the "masculine" to the "feminine" formula of sexuation that "Lacan accomplishes the passage from Law to Love, in short from Judaism to Christianity" (IR, 345). How does one arrive here from feminine atheist materialism?

First, for Žižek Christianity *is* the religion of atheism. He reads Christ's cry of dereliction as the "over-coming of metaphysics," i.e., the death of the big Other. What dies on the cross for Žižek is not so much God as the God of the beyond, the God of onto-theology, or, as Heidegger would put it, the god of the philosopher.[17] How then does this relate to Judaism and the formulae of sexuation? Simply put, Judaism *is* law: *Torah.* As such the Jewish God conforms to the structure of masculinity: the exception that grounds the rule. God is the big Other, outside of law, and hence unrepresentable within it, yet supportive of the law as a whole. Christianity, by contrast, is the religion of love. Christianity sus-pends those existing social symbolic networks of support (i.e., the law) in

---

17. Martin Heidegger, "The Onto-theo-logical Constitution of Metaphysics," in *Identity and Difference,* trans. Joan Stambaugh (San Francisco: Harper and Row, 1974), p. 72.

a moment of divine madness that Žižek identifies with love (agape). And by suspending the law, i.e., traversing the fantasy, Christianity brings the traumatic experience of immanence to bear upon its subject. As Žižek points out, "the Jewish God is the Real Thing of Beyond, while the divine dimension of Christ is just a tiny grimace, an imperceptible shade, which differentiates him from other (ordinary) humans" (PD, 80). In other words, the Jewish God is situated at the level of the impossible real (i.e., that excluded from the symbolic); whereas in Christ God is the real as impossible, so that what is traumatic about the incarnation is that what should remain veiled (Exod. 34:33-35) is unveiled (2 Cor. 3:13-16).

As Frederiek Depoortere has shown so lucidly, the transition from Judaism to Christianity follows a Hegelian trajectory in Žižek's work: "If Kant sought a religion within the bounds of reason alone, Hegel entirely agrees, except he also says reason has no bounds, and hence can take *within itself everything,* including religion. He does not betray the project of bringing religion within the bounds of reason, but by expanding reason, while claiming to complete Kant, he ends up with a more radical rationalization of religion: *there is no other to reason, there is no beyond, there is no transcendence.*"[18] How does this relate to Judaism or Christianity? Depoortere refers to Žižek's libidinal reading of the Jewish prohibition on images. As Žižek argues, the injunction against idolatry made no sense among the pagans, because it was already presupposed that any image would fall short of that which it represented; any image was *already* provision.

By contrast, the Jewish prohibition makes sense only on the assumption that such an image might actually render God *all too* visible. In other words, the Jewish prohibition is required not because God *is* transcendent, but the very opposite: God is *too* human (for example, in Genesis he appears to walk around the garden); the prohibition serves therefore as a "reaction formation" to Judaism's personalization of God, guarding against the traumatic experience of God as just another person.

Christianity completes this process of personalizing God "by asserting not only the likeness of God and man, but their direct *identity* in the

18. Frederiek Depoortere, "The End of God's Transcendence? On Incarnation in the Work of Slavoj Žižek," *Modern Theology* 23, no. 4 (2007): 497-523.

figure of Christ." Christianity brings the process set in motion by Judaism to its logical conclusion: it accepts God "as JUST ANOTHER HUMAN BEING, as a miserable man indiscernible from other humans with regard to his intrinsic properties" (OB, 130). In this way Christianity makes the transition from God as wholly Other to the Divine as "barely nothing," as the imperceptible "something" that makes Christ divine, the simple appearance of a thing that refuses to be grounded in some substantial property (OB, 130-31).

Žižek deepens the analysis of Christianity and feminine love with reference to Saint Paul's famous discussion of love in 1 Corinthians (13:1-13). As Žižek points out, Paul appears to make two seemingly contradictory claims: "First, St. Paul claims that there is love, even if we possess *all* knowledge" (IR, 334). In other words, even if we have all knowledge, there is still something that renders it incomplete. "Then, in the following paragraph, Paul claims that there is love only for *incomplete* beings, that is, beings possessing incomplete knowledge" (IR, 334). So, whereas in the first instance one is incomplete *without* love, in the second instance one is incomplete *with* love.

Now, if Saint Paul were following the logic of exception, he would be committed to saying the following: even if one had all knowledge, i.e., one was complete in the sense of belonging to the universal set, bearing the universal trait, etc., if one would gain love (i.e., the exception to the law), one would become complete. One would occupy the position as it were of the primal father, able to enjoy a pure unbounded *jouissance,* free from castration and untainted by sin. But Paul says something rather different. To receive and give love one must *be* incomplete, because the Christian attitude of love is one that involves a reflexive awareness of one's failings, a sense of humanity, etc. This is succinctly expressed in Paul's claim that one should boast not of one's strengths but of one's weaknesses (2 Cor. 11:30). Thus, Žižek reads Paul in the following way: *without love we are nothing, with love we actively become nothing.* "Love is not an exception to the field of knowledge but rather a 'nothing' that renders incomplete even the complete series or field of knowledge. . . . The Ultimate mystery of love is therefore that incompleteness is in a way higher that completion" (IR, 334-35). The parallel of love to Pauline femininity is therefore, and quite simply, this: femininity is challenging because it confronts masculinity with the possibility that we live in a world that is not supported by a big Other; i.e., there is no grounding exception. Pauline love is challenging because it identifies with love not at the level of the Ideal, i.e., the exception, but at the level of imperfection, the immanence of our being. We love not despite imperfection, but because of imperfection. This is a far cry from the claim that Paul is a misogynist who exhorts women not to speak in church. On Žižek's reading, Paul exhorts the church to adopt the very logic of femininity.

In all this one should not lose sight of the problematic juxtaposition Žižek offers between Judaism and Christianity — masculinity and femininity. What is one to make of such raw dichotomizing? Is Žižek offering a variant of the German feminist theologian Christian Mulack's thesis? In a book described as the "first anti-Semitic best-seller since 1945," she "blamed Nazism on Judaism, which she had identified as 'male' religion, in contrast to the 'female morality' of Jesus."[19] Certainly Žižek treats masculinity in a more pejorative sense by associating Jesus' attitude to the law with typically female ideas and the attitudes of the Pharisees and scribes with a typically male mental world, arguing that within patriarchy no man takes responsibility for his deeds because he acts on the command of someone higher.

But one should bear in mind the following. First, Žižek has always been a vocal critic of anti-Semitism. For example, in his early work he warns about the "dangerous proto-fascist potential"[20] of European anti-Semitism following the breakdown of communism and subsequent disappointment with democracy; and more recently he has critically engaged with the implicit anti-Semitic thrust of Richard Wolin's work, among others.[21] Second, one must read his thesis within the context of a sustained attempt to think through the problematic of anti-Semitism from a Lacanian perspective, so that what emerges is a far more compli-

19. Susannah Heschel, "Reading Jesus as a Nazi," in *A Shadow of Glory: Reading the New Testament after the Holocaust,* ed. Tod Linafelt (London: Routledge, 2002), pp. 27-41, 36.

20. Žižek, interviewed in *Lusitania* 4 (1994); http://www.lacan.com/perfume/ Žižekinter.htm (accessed August 19, 2007).

21. Žižek, "A Plea for a Return to *Différance* (with a Minor *Pro Domo Sua*)," *Critical Inquiry* 32 (2006): 226-49, 229.

cated approach that tries to do precisely that, complicate overly simplis-
tic models of anti-Semitism. For example, this is the basis of his criticisms
of Jean-Claude Milner's *Les penchants criminals de l'Europe démocratiqu*
(Paris: Éditions Verdier, 2003) (PV, 253-59). Third, Žižek has devoted con-
siderable words and time to develop a clearly defined theory of anti-
Semitism, which I discuss in some detail in chapter 5. Fourth, Žižek is
keen also to highlight the complex ways in which psychoanalysis is already a peculiarly Jewish science: "There is an overwhelming argument
for the intimate link between Judaism and psychoanalysis: in both cases,
the focus is on the traumatic encounter with the abyss of the desiring
Other, with the terrifying figure of an impenetrable Other who wants
something from us, but does not make it clear what this something is —
the Jewish people's encounter with their God whose impenetrable Call
disrupts the routine of human daily existence; the child's encounter with
the enigma of the Other's (in this case, parental) enjoyment" (L, 99).

Aquinas and *Jouissance*

In exploring the formulae of sexuation as the transition from old to new
law, we can refer back to Aquinas and his distinction between the two in
his discussion of the uses of ceremonial precepts. According to Aquinas,
under the old law there was a lack of truth (God was not revealed in the
incarnation); after Christ, i.e., under the new law, the truth revealed
through Christ is "superabundant [*excedentem*]" (*Summa Theologiæ* I-II,
q. 101, a. 2, r. 2); after the revelation in Christ there is *too much* truth, and
hence the lack arises from a prior plenitude.

How does this conform to the logic of masculinity and femininity?
Under the old law the perfect truth (i.e., the exception that formally organizes the need for ritual precepts and hence a worshiping community as
such) can only be grasped deficiently. Worshipers remain castrated; i.e.,
the perfect Truth is situated in an inaccessible area. However, under the
new law truth is *superabundant.* This is not to imply that what was formally thought of as perfect truth is even more perfect — that would be
tautological — but rather, perfect truth ceases to be found at one re-
move. Instead, truth is discovered here to be immanently discerned not

simply *in* creation, but as the very expression *of* creation. This is what makes truth *superabundant:* perfect truth ceases to establish a separate and contingent field of truth by excluding itself, allowing us to perceive it only through a veil; it *is* the very site of truth itself, one in which we are all implemented. In short, the challenge the new law presents to the old law is therefore the challenge the postmetaphysical logic of not-All brings to onto-theology.

In a similar fashion one can read the distinction between reason and faith in this way. Where the tendency has been to think of reason as masculine and faith as feminine, it is possible to rethink masculinity and femininity as *two modes of the relationship between reason and faith.* Where a masculine rationality is set against a feminine faith, one can always position them as either set apart — in such a way as to conform to the split between a public reason and a private faith — or coming together to form a complementary whole. By contrast, when reason and faith are viewed from the perspective of the masculine logic of exception and the feminine logic of not-All, one is faced with two different accounts of the antagonism that exists between the two. According to the logic of masculinity, reason and faith are related as the rule is to the exception. God is the exception (on the side of faith) who defines the rule (on the side of reason). This is the model adopted by Kierkegaard, for whom religion required a "leap into faith," i.e., the suspension of a universal rationality for the exception, i.e., God. In other words, rationality is castrated by the inaccessible real of God, who remains at a distance. By contrast, according to the logic of femininity, there is no exception to ground the rule. Rather, every exercise of rationality is already operative within the field of faith. Hence, it is not the case that one uses reason as a means of establishing proof by argument, but reason is the very proof itself, i.e., the fact that we are rational beings.

Žižek and New(er) Catholic Feminism

With this in mind, I propose to read Žižek *as a Catholic feminist.* By this I mean, first, that there are important overlaps between Žižek's project and that of the feminists; second, one can read Žižek in terms of the spe-

cific contribution Catholic feminism makes to his project. I shall begin
by saying something of the feminist/theological response to Freud.
Theologians have rightly highlighted the relation between religion and
the female sex in Freud's work. Their argument goes something like
this:[22] Freud did not always think of religion as sexually repressive; indeed, Freud's fear was the exact opposite: that religion gave dangerous license to sensual pleasure in the form of the religious experience. Religion was not sexually repressive but ought to be repressed because it was
sexual. This was part of his argument in *The Future of an Illusion* (SE,
21:64-65). In his initial debate with the French novelist Romain Rolland
(1866-1944), Freud argued that the true source of religious sentiment —
what Rolland called the *oceanic feeling* — was to be found in the wish fulfillment of the child, i.e., the desire for the undifferentiated bodily unity
with the mother (SE, 21:72). If Freud therefore discredited religion, it was
principally because it represented in part the body of the woman, which
Lacan replaced with language. In other words, Freud's rejection of religion was impelled by the law of castration, the founding law of culture.

The paradox was that the seeds of separation were to be found
within religion itself in the injunction against idolatry. The law led to the
rise of abstract thought, thereby enabling humanity to distinguish itself
from its sensual and feminine aspect. This was part of the argument in
Moses and Monotheism. Moses' injunction against idolatry was an advance in *Geistigkeit* (mind-spirit) because it introduced the abstract over
the sensual. As Freud says: "if this prohibition were accepted, it must
have had a profound effect. For it meant that a sensory perception was
given second place to what may be an abstract idea — a triumph of intel-
lectuality over sensuality or, strictly speaking, an instinctual renunciation, with all the necessary psychological consequences" (SE, 23:113).
Sensuality in general is sacrificed, and women's bodily experience in particular. Women were connected to a world men must smash in the move
from dependency to autonomy. This explains why the feminine is so
readily associated with the unconscious and the religious experience,
because culture is built on the repression of the female body.

22. See, for example, James Jones, *Religion and Psychology in Transition: Psychoanalysis, Feminism, and Theology* (New Haven and London: Yale University Press, 1996).

For this reason the left of Catholic feminism has been quick to embrace the postmetaphysical standpoint. For example, Tina Beattie describes her recent work *New Catholic Feminism* (2006) as "Heideggerian apophaticism, informed by the critical perspectives of the psycholinguistics and gender theory."[23] She, along with others like Grace Jantzen, welcomes the overcoming of metaphysics, perceiving less a descent into relativity — the masculine concern for truth — than a chance to recover the gendered and hence embodied female for Catholic life, such that it may be given ritual experience, i.e., representation within the priesthood. Her use of Heidegger underscores the link he made between embodied experience, religion, and the critique of onto-theology: beginning with the latter, Heidegger says: "Man can neither pray nor sacrifice to this god. Before the *causa sui*, man can neither fall to his knees in awe nor can he play music and dance before this god. The god-less thinking which must abandon the god of philosophy, god as *causa sui*, is thus perhaps closer to the divine God."[24]

In abandoning the God of metaphysics, we encounter a God who may be bodily worshiped; i.e., women are able to assume their role as women within religious liturgical, and sacramental, life, paradoxically becoming divine in the very act of overturning the traditional understanding of divinity (i.e., onto-theology) — by redefining its very meaning (i.e., politics proper).

However, as Beattie points out, Lacan, like Heidegger, was haunted by his Catholic heritage, yet resolutely rejected its promise of consolation, redemption, or hope in the face of death, determined instead to live in pursuit of a more authentic existence based upon an acceptance of the inevitability and finality of death. Hence it follows that, for Lacan and neo-Lacanians like Žižek, desire can only ever be focused on loss rather than satisfaction. This is why all desire is ultimately the desire for death,[25] a partial expression of the principal drive: the death drive (É, 719/848). The letter kills.

23. Tina Beattie, *New Catholic Feminism* (London and New York: Routledge, 2006), p. 9.

24. Heidegger, "Onto-theo-logical Constitution of Metaphysics," p. 72, in Beattie, *New Catholic Feminism*, p. 9.

25. Beattie, *New Catholic Feminism*, p. 197.

Nowhere is this more obvious than in Lacan's essay "God and ~~the~~ Woman's *Jouissance*," where the body disappears altogether when it comes to the field of sexual relations: "There is no chance for a man to have *jouissance* of a woman's body, otherwise stated, for him to make love, without castration" (SXX, 71-72). For Lacan, man's desire for a woman is not the desire for a bodily encounter as such; the encounter merely masks the impossibility of the sexual relation in the first place.

At this point we should return to Žižek's project to think through a materialist theology. Is this possible on the basis of Lacan if the material body is excluded, if it lacks a referent to the body, to the body in general and the female body in particular? It is not that Žižek is wrong, but that unless he endorses Catholic optimism in the transcendent and participating God, he risks paradoxically undermining his ability to think a properly materialist theology, i.e., a theology predicated upon the body (see chapter 2). In short, Žižek needs theology to prevent him from lapsing back into linguistic idealism.

This is also the argument of John Milbank: if you say there is only matter, matter turns into something rather mysterious and ethereal. We can say that it comprises atoms and the like, but it is a short step from there to a purely mathematical rendering of materiality. And likewise, while we can always simply point to the material objects that support us (the chair, our bodies, etc.), we still rely, as Bergson recognized, on one set of metaphors over another, such as hardness, duration, or solidity.

By contrast, Aquinas argues that matter is better suited than intellect to reflect the divine because it is simple, and thereby analogous to divine simplicity. In this way Aquinas gives sacramental validation to matter. Matter is not degenerate, as it was for the Gnostics, who favored the intellect; matter participates in and manifests the divine.

The logic is similar to Nietzsche's "History of an Error." When the supersensible world is destroyed, one is not left with a sensible world. No. In abolishing one, one abolishes the other because what is lost is the very distinction itself.[26] Likewise, in abolishing God we are not left with the material; the material too vanishes. Žižek's work seems to confirm

---

26. F. Nietzsche, *Twilight of the Idols/The Anti-Christ*, trans. R. Hollingdale (London: Penguin Books, 2003), pp. 50-51.

this when along with Lacan he argues that "the elevation to the status of symbolic authority has to be paid for by the death, murder even, of its empirical bearer" (ZR, vii).[27]

Can the problem be traced back to his misconstrued reading of Christ's cry of dereliction? May not the cry be reconfigured as the groan of desire because in God there is "an absence which is never nothing" — because its lack arrives from a prior plenitude — and "a presence that is never something" — because it cannot be refined in space and time but arises through the repeated unfolding of the sacrament by which material existence manifests the divine because it excels in its plenitude.[28]

There Is No Violent Relationship

Beattie's work is of particular interest because she reads the shift from the masculine logic onto-theology to postmetaphysical feminine in terms of Girard's distinction between myth and gospel, i.e., the contrast between a violent mimesis that breeds violence and the nonviolent mimesis of Christ that engenders peace. On this basis one can reread the formulae of sexuation in Girardian terms. For instance, to say *there is no sexual relation* is to say there is no unity between violent and nonviolent mimesis. This is not to say that violence has not been a defining factor in the historical emergence of the church or in its continued dealings with the world, nor that violence is not attested to in Scripture. It is to say rather that violence need not of itself become the presuppositional logic upon which a culture is founded, that there is an alternative logic identified as the not-All, which is not predicated upon a violent act of exclusion.

Extending this reading, one could say that under the old law the body was violently expelled, and in particular the female; under the new law each body is exceptional. The implications of this for Catholic theology could not be more critical when what is at stake is the representation of Christ by a male order of priests on the basis that Christ was biologically and ontologically a man. Such a relation has clearly been

27. "[T]he symbol first manifests itself as the killing of the thing" (É, 262/319).
28. Beattie, *New Catholic Feminism*, p. 197.

123

established along the imaginary axis, the specular image of Christ as man supporting the male priesthood.

How does one move from the identity with Christ's body to his representation by a male priesthood? From the perspective of masculinity, it is Christ's body as sexed that counts: Christ was a man; priests should be men, although the relation is as the rule to the exception: Christ was the perfect man, all priests are castrated. This is then transposed into the church: priests are not castrated — they have a privileged role in the Eucharist — but all laity are. By contrast, from the perspective of femininity, it is not that Christ was a man that counts, but that Christ was *uniquely* a man; the first man who was fully a man. Thus in the identity with his body it is not Christ *in his* particularity that counts (i.e., that he was biologically male); rather, it is the particularity itself (i.e., the fact that Christ was fully embodied).

As Beattie points out, Girard's scapegoat theory sheds further light on psychoanalysis that is applicable to Žižek. It is the nature of scapegoating that one masks the innocence of the victim, and hence the random nature of the sacrificial process. This is what Žižek would call the impotence of violence, violence that acts to mask castration rather than the violence incurred by a traumatic shift within the symbolic itself. The transgression imputed (i.e., the mask placed over the innocent) is often sexual in nature. Oedipus is a prime example of this. When Thebes suffers pestilence and drought, the cause is put down to Oedipus's sexual misdemeanor. Oedipus is violently expelled as the condition of social harmony. Yet as the narrative makes clear, the cause was clearly an arbitrary act of nature, plague, famine, etc., i.e., a cause that could not be supported by reference to a big Other; and the expulsion of Oedipus and the revival of the fortunes of Thebes merely confirm the system of sacrificial violence.

By maintaining the primacy of the sacrificial system, the church maintains the myth that sex and not death is the real problem.[29] As Beattie explains, this accounts for why the Catholic Church is "vehement and absolutist in its teachings with regard to sexuality and procreation, while it remains ambivalent with regard to violence and war."[30] This last point

29. Beattie, *New Catholic Feminism*, p. 188.
30. Beattie, *New Catholic Feminism*, p. 206.

is crucial. Our ability to confront the violence of sacrifice depends on our ability to confront the female body. What Beattie thereby avoids is reducing the body to the interest of identity politics while remaining exclusive of violence. The recovery of the female body in the Catholic Church would not simply be an addition to an existing structure; it would change fundamentally the nature of the structure, the political act par excellence.

CHAPTER 5

Enjoy Your Religion

One of Lacan's distinctive contributions to psychoanalysis has been to deepen the analysis of *jouissance,* or enjoyment, as Žižek likes to call it. Enjoyment is a central category of Oedipal dynamics: it is the desire to *enjoy* the mother that brings the child into conflict and rivalry with the father. And it is precisely enjoyment that is at stake in castration. As Lacan says: "Castration means that *jouissance* has to be refused" (É, 700/827). Lacan's twist was to highlight how the sense of a prior fullness of enjoyment from which one was subsequently removed (castration) was a myth, retroactively posited to hide the fact that there never was any enjoyment in the first place, or rather, that lack is constitutive of subjectivity. We begin, as it were, already begun. This was already implied in Freud's reworking of Darwin's primal horde. The ensuing guilt of the primal murder leads to a pact, which inaugurates the law manifest in the prohibition against murder and incest. Read from the perspective of *jouissance,* the prohibitions are not there to deny access to the females. They hide the fact that there never was access to the female (SVII, 176) and the group felt so guilty that it instigated the laws before the women could be enjoyed. This is why the very act serves in the end to strengthen the prohibition. Hence Lacan would say: "*Jouissance* is prohibited to whoever speaks, as such" (É, 696/821). Žižek translates *jouissance* as simply enjoyment, making it a far more amenable concept, employing it as a critical tool to explore the dynamics of law and culture (EYS, vii). Moreover, as Sarah Kay points out, the English has the advantage of gesturing toward the signified: enjoy-meant, i.e., enjoyment is always tainted by the signifier that establishes meaning *(meant)* over be-ing.[1]

Žižek takes as his starting point the injunctions and demands made on the consumer to *ENJOY!* Why put off for tomorrow what you can have today? For example, recent promotional ads on the packaging of Sainsbury's fruit simply state "Enjoy Summer!" On the surface, the demand to enjoy appears to transgress the law of castration (indulge yourself), yet as Žižek points out, this is not always the case; often the very demand to enjoy proves more of a prohibition than the prohibition of enjoyment itself. This same point was made by Kierkegaard about freedom and anxiety. Anxiety arose out of the awareness of "freedom's possibilities."[2] Anxiety is a response to the limitless possibilities that are open to us in our freedom, and pertains to salvation. In the task of becoming we can become anything, and while that can be an exhilarating experience, the choice and responsibility can also be crippling. So sometimes the best way to maintain order is to invite transgression of the law, i.e., complete freedom, because one ends up tyrannized by the very freedom itself. Hence Lacan says: "Nothing forces anyone to enjoy *(jouir)* except the super-ego. The super-ego is the imperative of jouissance — Enjoy!" (SXX, 3).

> "If God doesn't exist, then everything is prohibited" means the more you perceive yourself as an atheist, the more your unconscious is dominated by prohibitions that sabotage your enjoyment. (One should not forget to supplement this thesis with its opposite: if God exists, then everything is permitted — is this not the most succinct definition of the religious fundamentalist's predicament? For him, God fully exists, he perceives himself as His instrument, which is why he can do whatever he wants: his acts are redeemed in advance, since they express his divine will.) (L, 92)

So, law is maintained not simply by pressing the subject with guilt in the light of idealized order, but by its inverse, a voice that encourages the

---

1. Sarah Kay, *Žižek: A Critical Introduction* (Cambridge: Polity, 2003), p. 162.

2. Kierkegaard, *The Concept of Anxiety,* trans. R. Thomte (Princeton: Princeton University Press, 1980), p. 155.

transgression of the law through the demand to *enjoy*. Therefore one should not think of the law as simply a neat set of positive or negative prescriptions telling one what to do (e.g., love your neighbor; do not steal; etc.); rather, law operates in discrete and surprising ways, commanding enjoyment such that the freedom to enjoy becomes the obligation *to* enjoy and in doing so blocking access to enjoyment.

How does Žižek account for the paradoxical nature of law? Just as the subject is split between *the subject of the statement* (i.e., the speaking subject/symbolic) and *the subject of enunciation* (i.e., the unconscious/ real), so too the law is split, and thereby operates through both registers, the symbolic law with its publicly recognized statute and the superego imperative or demand to enjoy that operates in the register of the real, the realm of enjoyment, cutting through the symbolic but in such a way as to reinforce the legislative code. The two sides are therefore related, not unlike the Möbius strip or Klein bottle, in which two opposing surfaces seamlessly pass over into the other.

Enjoy Your Religion

In "Where Is Your Hamster?" Robert Pfaller explores the imperative to enjoy in the context of religion. As Pfaller explains, while ostensibly such a plea invites religious tolerance, the demand can also mask a far more insidious intolerance. What is at stake in the demand to enjoy is the difference between those who take religion far too seriously, living in an unreflected manner, and those who maintain a cynical distance, enjoying, without the fuss, aspects of the religious traditions that have helped structure their world. To say "I enjoy my religion" implies that I don't take it *too* seriously. To say "I enjoy . . ." is to emphasize one's ironical distance, so people will not assume we *really* believe. Žižek calls this ironic belief "decaffeinated belief" or "belief without belief."

It is not difficult to read this from the perspective of *jouissance*. Such ironic belief is sustained by the fantasy that once upon a time people really believed in an unreflective (uncastrated) manner — today's definition of fundamentalism — thereby creating the split between those who remain critical of their own tradition and those idiots who believe directly. The consequences of this logic are brilliantly summed up by Pfaller:

> Instead of joyfully indulging in an illusion, as for example in carnival practices, without bothering about its "true believers," we more and more reduce these joyful elements and care for making clear that it is not us who are the idiots. What characterises "decaffeinated belief" is therefore not an increase in fun *("Spass")*, but, on the contrary, a growing suspicion vis-à-vis joyful practices. . . . Alleged postmodern "hedonism" is, in fact, a reinforced anxiety to be regarded as naïve — a concern which testifies to an increasing lack of humour.[3]

This explains why Žižek is so scathing of postmodern liberal tolerance: it can become implicit in the very racism that it seeks to obviate. By urging the other to enjoy, it implicitly deprives the other of the critical edge. In religion it neutralizes the possibility of a religious critique of the economy by culturalizing religion, i.e., turning it into a set of culturally given practices within a more generalized economy. And because those practices are now seen as a marker of cultural differences, something given, they become beyond critique, they cannot be overcome, and therefore they must be tolerated. Not only is the religious critique of politics denied, but also any interreligious critique.[4]

Belief without Belief/The Inherent Transgression

The split in the law helps account for what Žižek calls the *inherent transgression* (PF, 18-27): a seeming act of transgression that acts to reinforce the very thing it critiques. Žižek exemplifies this point in *On Belief* with reference to the way Western Buddhism presents itself as a remedy for capitalist dynamics, encouraging us to "uncouple and retain inner

3. Robert Pfaller, "Where Is Your Hamster? The Concept of Ideology in Žižek's Cultural Theory," in *Traversing the Fantasy: Critical Responses to Slavoj Žižek*, ed. G. Boucher, J. Glynos, and M. Sharpe (Aldershot: Ashgate, 2005), pp. 105-24, 120.

4. For example, it is far easier to reduce Islam to a set of cultural practices to be enjoyed than to stand under its judgment over our current English laws on gambling publicity.

peace" (OB, 12) while functioning all the while as an ideological supplement: "Instead of trying to cope with the accelerating rhythm of technological progress and social changes, one should rather renounce the very endeavour to regain control over what goes on, rejecting it as the expression of the modern logic of domination — one should instead 'let oneself go,' drift along, while retaining an inner distance towards the mad dance of this accelerated process" (OB, 12-13). In this way one is enabled "to fully participate in the frantic pace of the capitalist game while sustaining the perception you are not really in it" (OB, 15). In capitalism, Buddhism, the antimaterialist doctrine par excellence, finds itself in support of the most materialist of economic ideologies. However, it should be recalled that Buddhism arose out of a political critique of the Hindu caste system. Thus from its inception Buddhism was a material and politically engaged movement, and so to remain within the spirit of Buddhism is not to abandon a political critique but its opposite: only by engaging in the political critique does one make a good Buddhist.

How, then, does one account for the inherent transgression? As Žižek explains, the problem is that law is not experienced as natural or spontaneous, but imposed (FA, 142). Law involves what Lacan calls the *Vel* of alienation, the forced choice between being and meaning. If we choose being, the subject disappears, it eludes us, and it falls into nonmeaning; if we choose meaning, it survives but "it emerges in the field of the Other, to be in a large part of its field, eclipsed by the disappearance of being, induced by the very function of the signifier" (SXI, 211). So it is not the case that law is sometimes obeyed and at other times is not; rather, the law is *"always-already mediated by the (repression of the) desire to transgress the Law."* And this accounts for guilt. When we obey law, we do so over and against the more primary desire to transgress it, and so "the more we obey the law, the more we *are* guilty because this obedience, in effect, *is* a defence against sinful desire" (FA, 142).

Enjoy Your Neighbor's Religion

In *Tarrying with the Negative* Žižek employs Lacanian psychoanalysis to explore the question of racist nationalism in an attempt to rethink those "elementary notions about national identification" (TN, 200).[5] What holds a given community together, he argues, cannot be reduced to the symbolic, i.e., a positive figurehead, team, object, etc. Rather, what holds any given unity together is a relation to *das Ding* (the Thing). When Lacan employs this term, he does so with shades of both Kant's "thing-in-itself," a negative entity not accessible in terms of positive identification but necessarily posited as a condition of experience, and Heidegger's essay of the same name: "Das Ding."[6] Here Heidegger famously describes a vase, giving attention to the void or absence *(das Ding)* around which the vase has been fashioned. A central lack is constitutive of the vase as a [w]hole. A vase is never empty, because when it is without water or milk it literally contains nothing. And it is against this negative background that being emerges. Heidegger tempers the transcendental element in Kant. What is at stake in any given community is not some *noumenal* truth that transcendentally secures those sets of relations within the real world — the metaphysical standpoint — but the immanent inertia of the real, the void around which subjectivity and community are constituted. As Žižek says: "National identification is by definition sustained by a relationship towards the Nation qua *Thing*" (TN, 201).

And it is because community is constituted by this negative entity that nationalism, and by extension one might speak also of a religious sense of pride, often takes a contradictory form. As Žižek explains, "It appears to us as 'our Thing' . . . as something accessible only to us, as something 'they,' the others, cannot grasp; nevertheless it is something constantly menaced by 'them'" (TN, 201). For a nation, religion, or community, to believe in their thing is not to believe in a collection of common features that unite the group but to believe in the possibility of belief itself; one believes because others believe, or *man's belief is the belief of the other*. But the belief itself is without an object of intentionality. As Žižek explains with reference to Christianity: "The Holy Spirit *is* the community of believers in which Christ lives after his death: *to believe in Him equals believing in belief itself*" (TN, 202).

5. See also "The Nation Thing" (LA, 162-70).

6. M. Heidegger, "The Thing," in *Poetry, Language, Thought,* trans. Albert Hofstadter (New York: Harper and Row, 1975), pp. 163-86.

This is why Žižek resists reducing an eruption of national sentiment to the performative effect of the given discursive operation, such as the effect of the media.[7] Rather, a "substance" (TN, 202) must be added, which psychoanalysis calls "enjoyment" *(jouissance)*. There must always be "the remainder of some *real,* non-discursive kernel, what psychoanalysis calls enjoyment *(jouissance)* which must be present for the Nation qua discursive entity-effect to achieve its ontological consistency" (a case of the nothing as something!) (TN, 202). This is precisely what is at stake in racism because it is the real that interpellates one into the existing social fabric:

> What is therefore at stake in ethnic tensions is always the possession of the national Thing. We always impute to the "other" an excessive enjoyment: he wants to steal our enjoyment (by ruining our way of life) and/or he has access to some secret, perverse enjoyment. In short what really bothers us about the "other" is the peculiar way he organises his enjoyment, precisely the surplus, the "excess" that pertains to this way: the smell of "their" food, "their" noisy songs and dances, "their" strange manners, "their" attitude to work. (TN, 202-3)

Again, there is a phantasmic and mythical construction at work here, not unlike Freud's primal horde, in which the theft of enjoyment is posited to hide the traumatic fact that the nation never possessed the thing in the first place: loss is original and constitutive; enjoyment only arises precisely through being left behind (TN, 203-4).

Anti-Semitism

For Žižek the libidinal economy of racism takes no greater precedence than in the issues surrounding anti-Semitism, what Žižek refers to as

7. A good example of the performative effect of the media is the fatwa surrounding the publication of Salman Rushdie's *The Satanic Verses*. The initial burning of the book in Bolton on December 2, 1988, passed away quite peacefully. Only later, on January 14, 1989, when, on the advice of a solicitor, they restaged the book burning in Bradford for the media, did the international community of Muslims respond.

"the purest incarnation of ideology as such" (SOI, 125). How does Žižek read the figure of the Jew qua ideology? Given his claim that fantasy does not obscure reality, it is constitutive of reality, the approach to anti-Semitism cannot be within the order of objectivity, i.e., of learning "to see Jews as they really are." Instead, one must ask the question concerning how we "have constructed this figure to escape a certain deadlock of our desire" (SOI, 48).

The traditional Freudian approach to any given figure of a "Jew" is to show how the "Jew" is operative according to the mechanisms of the dreamwork: displacement and condensation; reading the ideological expression of a "Jew" in terms of our unconscious desire. Žižek does just this in *The Sublime Object of Ideology*. "First there is displacement: the basic trick of anti-semitism is to displace social antagonism between the sound social texture, social body, and the Jew as the force corroding it, the force of corruption. Thus it is not society itself which is 'impossible,' based on antagonism — the source of corruption is located in a particular entity, the Jew" (SOI, 125). Second, there is condensation: "the figure of the Jew condenses opposing features, features associated with lower and upper classes. Jews are supposed to be dirty *and* intellectual, voluptuous *and* impotent, and so on" (SOI, 125). On the basis of these operations one can expose the Jew as "a symptom in the sense of a coded message, a cypher, a disfigured representation of social antagonisms; by undoing this work of displacement/condensation, we can determine its meaning" (SOI, 126).

However, as Žižek explains, such an approach does not account for the way the figure of the "Jew" captures our desire. In other words, we need to account for anti-Semitism not in terms of meaning but in terms of enjoyment.

> To penetrate its [anti-Semitism's] fascinating force, we must take into account the way "Jew" enters the framework of fantasy structuring our enjoyment. Fantasy is basically a scenario filling out the empty space of a fundamental impossibility, a screen masking a void. . . . [S]ociety is always traversed by an antagonistic split which cannot be integrated into the symbolic order. And the stake of social-ideological fantasy is to construct a vision of society which *does* exist, a society

which is not split by an antagonistic division, a society in which the relation between its parts is organic, complementary. The clearest case
is, of course, the corporatist vision of Society as an organic Whole, a
social Body in which the different classes are like extremities, members each contributing to the Whole according to its function — we
may say that "Society as a corporate Body" is the fundamental ideological fantasy. How then do we take account of the distance between
this corporatist vision and the factual society split by antagonistic
struggles? The answer is, of course, the Jew: an external element, a foreign body introducing corruption into the social fabric. . . . The notion
of social fantasy is therefore a necessary counterpart to the concept of
antagonism: fantasy is precisely the way the antagonistic fissure is
masked. In other words, *fantasy is a means for an ideology to take its
own failure into account in advance.* . . . Jews are clearly a social symptom: the point at which the immanent social antagonism assumes a
positive form, erupts on to the social surface, the point at which it becomes obvious that society doesn't work. (SOI, 126-27)

In other words, the "Jew" embodies "a certain blockage" standing in as
the signifier of the impossibility of signification (what Lacan called the
objet petit a, the object cause of our desire, i.e., the very sign that signifies
the impossibility of society representing itself to itself in its full identity
as a closed homogenous totality). Hence, "far from being the positive
cause of social negativity, *the 'Jew' is a point at which social negativity as
such assumes positive existence*" (SOI, 127).

For Lacan the lack within the signifier, i.e., the fact that no amount of
signification is possible to ensure a "complete description" of a given
thing, returns as a question: *Che vuoi?* What do you want? Žižek contends that anti-Semitism is a response to this fundamental structural
problem: "[I]n the anti-Semitic perspective, the Jew is precisely a person
about whom it is never clear 'what he really wants' — that is, his actions
are always suspected of being guided by some hidden motives (the Jewish conspiracy, world domination and the moral corruption of Gentiles,
and so on)" (SOI, 114). So, given the anti-Semite's paranoid fantasy of a
Jewish plot, the point is not to ask the objective question, nor is it to assume that we simply project disavowed aspects of society onto a foreign

other: "The 'conceptual Jew' cannot be reduced to the externalisation of my (anti-Semite's) 'inner conflict': on the contrary, it bears witness to (and tries to cope with) the fact that I am originally decentred, part of an opaque network whose meaning and logic elude my control" (PF, 9). This is compounded in Judaism for precisely theological reasons: "Is not the Jewish God the purest embodiment of this *Che vuoi?*," of the desire of the Other in its terrifying abyss, with the formal prohibition to "make an image of God" — to fill out the gap of the Other's desire with a positive fantasy (SOI, 115)? The goal therefore in confronting anti-Semitism is not to raise the objective question but to traverse the social fantasy by "identity[ing] with the symptom," i.e., "the point at which the imminent social antagonism assumes a positive form" (SOI, 127): "to recognize in the 'excesses,' in the disruptions of the 'normal' way of things, the key offering us access to its true functioning. This is similar to Freud's view that the keys to the functioning of the human mind were dreams, slips of the tongue, and similar abnormal phenomena" (SOI, 128). Žižek's approach is not without criticism. For example, Claudia Breger has argued that by associating the figure of the Jew primarily with the real (i.e., without form or shape), he perpetuates the status of the Jew within Western discourse as the figure of lack, a process she calls "othering" the Jew.[8] So, while Žižek remains nonetheless critical of the Nazi attempt to "seize, measure, [and] change into a positive property enabling us to identify Jews in an objective way" (SOI, 97), he fails to bring into question his initial assumption that the Jew is not a positive entity in the first place (a criticism Breger also applies to his treatment of women).

But Žižek achieves something that is missing in Breger's criticism. By interpreting the issue of anti-Semitism through the lens of Lacan, he does not so much perpetuate the Jew as lack as *subvert* such readings, because the figure of the Jew is made to bear witness to the fact that we are all originally decentered, lacking, and eluding control.

Moreover, Breger goes too far when she criticizes Žižek for analyzing an anti-Semitic joke. It would have been acceptable had she merely disagreed on *how* he analyzed the joke, but she contended that analyzing an

8. Claudia Breger, "The Leader's Two Bodies: Slavo Žižek's Postmodern Political Theology," *Diacritics* 31, no. 1 (2001): 73-90, 83.

anti-Semitic joke in the first place made the joke worthy of reflection and thus compounded anti-Semitic sentiments. According to Breger, its very presence somehow reinforced anti-Semitism by "reiterating . . . [the Jew's] necessary place in the symbolic order."[9] Yet her paper ignores precisely that — any detailed engagement with his analysis of the anti-Semitic joke. Instead, her condemnation silences the debate by relieving the reader of the need to critically explore and understand motivating factors in anti-Semitic jokes that continue to surface or "slip" out in everyday and extraordinary ways.[10]

Too Much Religion

In his "Names-of-the-Father" seminar Lacan brings the themes of *jouissance,* anxiety, and desire to bear on Caravaggio's *Sacrifice of Isaac,* providing, as it were, a reading of the *Akeidah.* In a very different reading to Žižek's, what counts for Lacan is not so much the "suspension of the symbolic" as the initiation *of* the symbolic. Lacan comments on the painting:

> Here may be marked the knife blade separating God's bliss from what in that tradition is presented as his desire. The thing whose downfall it is a matter of provoking is biological origin. That is the key to the mystery, in which may be read the aversion of the Jewish tradition concerning what exists everywhere else. The Hebrew hates the metaphysico-sexual rites which unite in celebration the community to God's erotic bliss. He accords special value to the gap separating desire and fulfilment. The symbol of that gap we find in the same context of El Shadday's relation to Abraham, in which, primordially, is born the law of circumcision, which gives as a sign of the covenant between the peo-

9. Breger, "The Leader's Two Bodies," p. 83.

10. A Sky News reporter recently apologized after a live microphone accidentally left on broadcast his live reaction to David Cameron's speech on immigration policy. The presenter joked on air that the Conservatives favored a policy of "extermination" for immigrants. http://www.timesonline.co.uk/tol/news/politics/article2767170.ece (accessed October 30, 2007).

ple and the desire of he who has chosen them what? — that little piece of flesh sliced off.

It is with that *petit a,* to whose introduction I had led you last year, along with a few hieroglyphics bearing witness to the customs of the Egyptian people, that I shall leave you. (NoF, 94)

Lacan relates anxiety to the experience of an unbounded *jouissance,* i.e., God's "bliss"; the knife stands for the cut induced by the signifier upon subjectivity, the ritual beginning that spares the child the anxiety of the mother's *jouissance,* opening up instead the economy of desire. The knife wielded by Abraham stands on the threshold between *jouissance* and desire. Or, as Charles Shepherdson puts it:

> Anxiety is thus present in the moment when Abraham is prepared to sacrifice everything to an inscrutable and apparently insatiable Other, whose appetite knows no limit, and demands everything of the subject; and this anxiety is transformed, channelled in the direction of desire, but the pact of symbolic law precisely when God refuses to let this sacrifice occur, putting the ram in place of Isaac, and thereby establishing a new relation to the Other, in which God's desire is no longer confused with his devouring *jouissance* that the subject must somehow appease. We thereby see more clearly how anxiety is situated by Lacan as the threshold that the subject must cross on the way toward desire amid the symbolic mediation.[11]

How does this compare with Freud's account of anxiety? Freud's own thought may be said to follow two phases, although these two phases contain a variety of interpretive nuances. In his early work he accounts for anxiety in terms of an excessive libidinal tension and its inadequate discharge (i.e., too much phallic enjoyment) (SE, 1:191); what some detractors reduce to a "pipe and valve" theory.[12] In his later work, however, Freud shifted his understanding of anxiety to the level of the ego: "the

---

11. Charles Shepherdson, foreword to *Lacan's Seminar on "Anxiety": An Introduction,* by Roberto Harari, trans. Jane Lamb-Ruiz (New York: Other Press, 2001), p. xxxii.

12. Shepherdson, foreword, p. xix.

ego is the actual seat of anxiety" (SE, 20:140). On this account, anxiety is the result of a threat to the ego, of which the primary instance is the threat of separation or loss: "Anxiety appears as a reaction to the felt loss of the object; and we are at once reminded of the fact that castration anxiety, too, is a fear of being separated from a highly valued object, and that the earliest anxiety of all — the 'primal anxiety' of birth — is brought about on the occasion of a separation from the mother" (SE, 20:137). It is from this latter perspective that the ground of anxiety shifts from the somatic to the psychic disposition of the subject, becoming tied to primal loss rather than an excess of libido, hence Freud argues that it is anxiety (the anxiety of separation) that creates repression, and *not* repression that creates anxiety (the buildup of libidinal excitement).

Lacan's return to Freud represents a radicalization of this latter inflection, while returning to aspects of Freud's first account. In Lacan's reading of Freud, it is not the lack that arises from separation that gives rise to anxiety, but the *lack of that lack*, i.e., when one fails to make the *cut* of the symbolic and is invaded instead by the primacy of *jouissance:* the lethal excess of enjoyment. On this account, anxiety is not an aspect of the ego's frailty for which the cure would be to develop stronger defenses; anxiety concerns "the very birth of the subject as such";[13] anxiety is the existential plenitude upon which life is played out.

All of this allows for an alternative take on the *Akeidah.* The problem arises because Abraham's experience of God's bliss is the problem of being "affected by the desire of the Other" (NoF, 82). God desired Isaac not all the while knowing in the manner of some secret self-understanding that he would stay Abraham's hand at the final moment; *God desired Isaac because he wanted what Abraham most desired:* desire is the desire of the Other. In other words, desire is always mediated, it is never simply our desire but is shaped through imaginary, or what Girard would call mimetic, patterns of rivalry. Hence it is only in the final throes of the sacrificial gesture when God realizes that Abraham *will* readily sacrifice Isaac, that God puts an end to the spectacle, because if Abraham will readily cede his most cherished son, that cannot be it *(ça);* Abraham's desire *must* lie elsewhere.

13. Shepherdson, foreword, p. lxi.

The knife will spare the child. So from where does anxiety arise? Anxiety is experienced as the overbearing proximity of God, his voice, pressing upon Abraham as demand. And Abraham's sacrifice exemplifies the means by which demand is transfigured through ritual into desire. Here Žižek's reading parts company with Lacan. What matters for Žižek is the fidelity to this singular demand in contravention of the socio-symbolic. This is really Kierkegaard's point: the religious stage (i.e., the real) is higher than the ethical (i.e., the symbolic). And it is by invocation of the real that the symbolic is brought into question. By contrast, Lacan places the emphasis on the transition from the real to the symbolic; he highlights the logic of symbolic castration by which desire is put to play in the establishment of ritual order. In short, castration spares one from having to respond to that unbearable *jouissance*.

Three points: first of all, one should recall Aquinas's point regarding ceremonial precepts here (see chapter 2). The Eucharist is not there primarily to maintain a link to God as if God were generally distanced and aloof and required a little cajoling to come to the table; the rituals testify to the too-muchness of God; the sacraments are in one sense a defense *against* God because of his superabundance. This is why the atheist is misguided in thinking that unbelief is the only credible response to the problem of God; if you really want to be free of God, then religion is geared specially to that end. Freud also made this point in his account of religious experience: religious ritual (i.e., law) is a defense against the *jouissance* of the mother, what Freud identified as the *oceanic* experience. So Freud linked a direct religious experience to the excess of *jouissance* associated with the mother from which the Oedipal law and castration render life. In short, the religious cut is a defense against God's *jouissance*.

The second point concerns Girard. Lacan prefaces his reading with the very point Girard makes: the *Akeidah* stages the historical necessity of God and the angels to intervene in putting an end to the violence of sacrifice. "Before waxing emotional, as is customary on such occasion, we might remember that sacrificing one's little boy to the local *Elohim* was quite common at the time — and not only at that time, for it continued so late that it was constantly necessary of the Angel of the Name, or the prophet speaking in the name of the Name to stop the Israelites, who were about to start it again" (NoF, 92). In doing so, Lacan inadvertently provides an argument in favor of God by stating that he exceeds the conditions; he also provides in advance the basis for a more thorough reading of his work in the light of Girard. For example, one might say the transition from *jouissance* to desire describes the transition from violence to nonviolence.

Third, one should note the conservatism of Lacan's reading. The story restages the initiation of the symbolic; the cut of the blade opens up signification, yet language serves as a defense against the bliss of unguarded *jouissance,* just as for Freud religion was justified to the extent that it held in check socially harmful instincts (SE, 9:124-25).

From *Theo-logie* to *Dio-logie*

In 1963 the Société Française de Psychanalyse, a splinter group of analysts to which Lacan belonged, was, after much petition, accepted into the fold of the International Psychoanalytical Association on the condition that "Dr. Lacan is no longer recognised as a training analyst" (T, 79). Lacan had promised that year to present a series of seminars on the Names-of-the-Father, but in the light of these events the course never appeared, except for an initial lecture collected in *Television.* More recently Jacques-Alain Miller has speculated over the content of that "inexistent" seminar. What might Lacan have said on the matter? Drawing upon scattered references, Miller starts to give shape to this spectral seminar.

We can follow Miller's lead. The first clue is a quote from "Science and Truth": "I am inconsolable at having had to drop my project of relating the function of the name-of-the-Father to the study of the Bible" (É, 743/874). As Miller points out, "this phrase contains a very precise indication on the aim of the inexistent Seminar. . . . The process was to relate its function [i.e., the Name-of-the-Father] to the study of the Bible."[14] According to Miller, Lacan's aim was to show how the Name-of-the-Father stems from a tradition that is both Greek and Jewish. In other words, he

14. Jacques-Alain Miller, "The Inexistent Seminar," trans. Philip Dravers, *Psychoanalytic Notebooks* 15 (2005): 9-42, 25.

was set to pose Tertullian's question in the light of psychoanalysis: What has Athens got to do with Jerusalem; Moses with Oedipus, the two traditions upon which Christianity and psychoanalysis are built?

This distinction was later captured in "Méprise du sujet supposé savoir" (AÉ, 329-40), where Lacan comes up with the neologism *dio-logie* as distinct from *theo-logie.* The distinction corresponds to the Latin *(Dio)* and Greek *(Theo)* derivations for God. How do we understand this distinction?

Lacan's preference for *dio-logie* highlights his tendency to widen psychoanalysis out into the Christian field, from Jerusalem to Rome. Rome holds a double significance here, because the language is Latin, yet Latin itself was not the language of the Christian sources, so Latin implies a tradition that includes the idea of interpretation, and hence translation.

Lacan also links *theo-logia* to *theoria,* and hence metaphysics. This is made more explicit through the association Lacan draws between *theo-logia* and the *subject supposed to know* (a position closely identified with the metaphysical standpoint; see chapter 1), and *dio-logia* to the Name-of-the-Father.

What we encounter in Lacan, therefore, seems to urge the shift away from metaphysics and onto-theology, ironically, toward God the Father, where the Name-of-the-Father functions not as a new *theoria* but as the cut of signifier that spares the subject from anxiety. *Dio-logia* is therefore a discourse not on God as subject-supposed-to-know, but on the God of the object, small *a,* i.e., the object of desire; or rather, the condition *of* desire that sets in motion the very principle of difference. One could draw here upon G. K. Chesterton as Žižek has recently: "all modern philosophies are chains which connect and fetter; Christianity is a sword which separates and sets free. No other philosophy makes God actually rejoice in the separation of the universe into living souls."[15]

To underline the importance of *dio-logia* for psychoanalysis, Lacan says the following: "Without this marked place, psychoanalysis would be reduced to what is for the best and for the worse, a delusion of Schreberien kind" (AÉ, 337). In other words, just as psychoanalysis relies on the Oedipus complex to meaningfully configure the art of psycho-

15. G. K. Chesterton, *Orthodoxy* (San Francisco: Ignatius, 1995), p. 139.

analysis, so also psychoanalysis falls into delusion without the Jewish/ Christian legacy; hence psychoanalysis requires theology, and Lacan's nonexistent seminar had that intention of "recalling the fact that the first of the Names-of-the-Father is God-the-Father — that behind the Father of Oedipus is God the Father."[16]

But why exactly did Lacan not push to make this a seminar topic, if not during those turbulent years then at least later? Again, from "Méprise du sujet supposé savoir" (AÉ, 329-40): "The place of God-the-Father is the one I designate as the Name-of-the-Father. I wanted to develop it in what should have been the thirteenth year of my Seminar . . . when a passage to the act on the part of my psychoanalyst colleagues forced me to bring it to a close after its first lesson. I will never take up this theme again, seeing in this the sign that psychoanalysis is not ready for this seal to be lifted" (AÉ, 337). What is one to make of this remarkable claim? Perhaps we should allow Miller to be our guide: "To return to the study of the Bible (Lacan's declared ambition) is to return to the lush pastures of the original tradition to which we owe the Name-of-the-Father . . . a return to the Bible as the kernel of what supported Freud himself as the inheritor of this tradition."[17] The popularity of Žižek's work suggests in no small measure that psychoanalysis is ready for the seal to be lifted such that it may take up again the legacy of the Bible. To do so would be to engage Žižek's work at its most critical, because it would mean taking him absolutely seriously when he says Christianity really *is* worth saving.

---

16. Miller, "The Inexistent Seminar," p. 25.
17. Miller, "The Inexistent Seminar," p. 27.

The Counterbook of Christianity

Slavoj Žižek

What can I add to the book that provides a precise critical reading of my continuous struggle to come to terms, as an atheist, with our Christian legacy? The only honest thing to do is to "dot the *i*," as it were, with a concise version of what I perceive as the Communist core of the Christian ethical revolution.

Let me begin with a simple mental experiment with two of Hitchcock's late masterpieces. What if *Vertigo* were to end after Madeleine's suicide, with the devastated Scottie listening to Mozart in the sanatorium? What if *Psycho* were to end seconds prior to the shower murder, with Marion staring into the falling water, purifying herself? In both cases we would get a consistent short film. *Vertigo* would be a drama of the destruction caused by the violently obsessive male desire: it is the very excessive-possessive nature of male desire that makes it destructive of its object — (male) love is murder, as Otto Weininger knew long ago. *Psycho* would be a moral tale about a catastrophe prevented in the last minute: Marion commits a minor crime, escaping with the stolen money to rejoin her lover; on the way she meets Norman, who is like a figure of moral warning, rendering visible to Marion what awaits her at the end of the line if she follows the path taken; this terrifying vision sobers her up, so she withdraws to her room, plans her return, and then takes a shower, as if to cleanse her of her moral dirt. In both cases, it is thus as if what we are first lured into taking as the full story is all of a sudden displaced, reframed, relocated into, or supplemented by another story, something along the lines of the idea envisaged by Borges in the opening story of his

Fictions, which culminates in the claim: "Un libro que no encierra su contra-libro es considerado incompleto" [A book which does not contain its counterbook is considered incomplete]. In his 2005-2006 seminar, Jacques-Alain Miller elaborated on this idea, referring to Ricardo Piglia.[1] Piglia quoted as an example of Borges's claim one of Mikhail Chekhov's tales whose nucleus is: "A man goes to the casino at Monte Carlo, wins a million, returns to his place and commits suicide."

If this is the nucleus of a story, one must, in order to tell it, divide the twisted story in two: on the one hand, the story of the game; on the other, that of the suicide. Thus Piglia's first thesis: that a story always has a double characteristic and always tells two stories at the same time, which provides the opportunity to distinguish the story that is on the first plane from the number 2 story that is encoded in the interstices of story number 1. We should note that story number 2 appears only when the story is concluded, and it has the effect of surprise. What joins these two stories is that the elements, the events, are inscribed in two narrative registers that are at the same time distinct, simultaneous, and antagonistic, and the construction itself of the story is supported by the junction between the two stories. The inversions that seem superfluous in the development of story number 1 become, on the contrary, essential in the plot of story number 2.

There is a modern form of the story that transforms this structure by omitting the surprise finale without closing the structure of the story, which leaves a trace of a narrative, and the tension of the two stories is never resolved. This is what one considers as being properly modern: the subtraction of the final anchoring point that allows the two stories to continue in an unresolved tension.

This is the case, says Piglia, with Hemingway, who pushed the ellipse to its highest point in such a way that the secret story remains hermetic. One perceives simply that there is another story that needs to be told but remains absent. There is a hole. If one modified Chekhov's note in Hemingway's style, it would not narrate the suicide, but rather the text would be assembled in such a way that one might think that the reader already

---

1. Piglia's text to which Miller refers without providing any references is "Tesis sobre el cuento," *Revista Brasileira de Literatura Comparada* 1 (1991): 22-25.

knew it. Kafka constitutes another of these variants. He narrates very simply, in his novels, the most secret story, a secret story that appears on the first plane, told as if coming from itself, and he encodes the story that should be visible but becomes, on the contrary, enigmatic and hidden.[2]

Back to Hitchcock's *Vertigo* and *Psycho*. Is this not precisely the structure of the narrative twist/cut in both films? In both cases story number 2 (the shift to Judy and to Norman) appears only when the story seems concluded, and it certainly has the effect of surprise; in both cases the two narrative registers are at the same time distinct, simultaneous, and antagonistic, and the construction itself of the story is supported by the junction between the two stories. The inversions that seem superfluous in the development of story number 1 (like the totally contingent intrusion of the murdering monster in *Psycho*) become essential in the plot of story number 2.

One can thus well imagine, along these lines, *Psycho* remade by Hemingway or Kafka. Exemplary of Hemingway's procedure is "The Killers," his best-known short story that, on a mere ten pages, reports in a terse style the arrival of two killers to a small provincial city; they occupy there a diner, awaiting a mysterious "Swede" whom they have to kill. Swede's young friend escapes from the diner and informs him that two killers are on the way to murder him, yet Swede is so desperate and resigned that he sends the boy off and calmly awaits them. The "second story," the explanation of this enigma (what happened to Swede that he is ready to calmly await his death), is never told. (The classic film noir based on this story tries to fill in this void: in the series of flashbacks, the "second story," the betrayal of a femme fatale, is told in detail.) In Hemingway's version, Norman's story will remain hermetic: the spectator will simply perceive that there is another (Norman's) story that needs to be told but remains absent — there is a hole. In Kafka's version Norman's story would appear in the first plane, told as if coming from itself: Norman's weird universe would have been narrated directly, in the first person, as something most normal, while Marion's story would have been encoded/enframed by Norman's horizon, told as enigmatic and hidden. Just imagine the conversation between Marion and Norman in his private room, prior to the shower

2. Jacques-Alain Miller, "Profane Illuminations," *Lacanian Ink* 28 (2007): 12-13.

murder: the way we have it now, our point of identification is Marion, and Norman appears as a weird and threatening presence. What if this scene were reshot with Norman as our point of identification, so that Marion's "ordinary" questions would appear as what they often effectively are, a cruel and insensitive intrusion into Norman's world?

This is how, from a proper Hegelo-Lacanian perspective, one should subvert the standard self-enclosed linear narrative: not by means of a postmodern dispersal into a multitude of local narratives, but by means of its redoubling in a hidden counternarrative. (This is why the classic detective whodunit is so similar to the psychoanalytic process: in it, also, the two narrative registers — the visible story of the discovery of crime and its investigation by the detective, and the hidden story of what really happened — are "at the same time distinct, simultaneous, and antagonistic, and the construction itself of the story is supported by the junction between the two stories.") And is one of the ways to conceptualize class struggle not also such a split between the two narratives that are "at the same time distinct, simultaneous, and antagonistic, and the construction itself of the story is supported by the junction between the two stories"? If one starts to tell the story from the standpoint of the ruling class, one sooner or later reaches a gap, a point at which something arises that doesn't make sense within the horizon of this story, something experienced as a meaningless brutality, something akin to the unexpected intrusion of the murdering figure in the shower scene from *Psycho*. In 1922 the Soviet government organized the forced expulsion of leading anti-Communist intellectuals, from philosophers and theologians to economists and historians. They left Russia for Germany on a boat known as the "Philosophy Steamer." Prior to his expulsion, Nikolai Lossky, one of those forced into exile, enjoyed with his family the comfortable life of the haute bourgeoisie, supported by servants and nannies. He "simply couldn't understand who would want to destroy his way of life. What had the Losskys and their kind done? His boys and their friends, as they inherited the best of what Russia had to offer, helped fill the world with talk of literature and music and art, and they led gentle lives. What was wrong with that?"[3]

---

3. Lesley Chamberlain, *The Philosophy Steamer: Lenin and the Exile of the Intelligentsia* (London: Atlantic Books, 2006), pp. 23-24.

To account for such a foreign element, one has to pass to "story number 2," the story from the standpoint of the exploited. For Marxism, class struggle is not the all-encompassing narrative of our history, it is an irreducible clash of narratives — and does the same not go for today's Israel? Many peace-loving Israelis confess to their perplexity: they just want peace and a shared life with Palestinians; they are ready to make concessions, but why do Palestinians hate them so much, why the brutal suicide bombings that kill innocent wives and children? The thing to do here is of course to supplement this story with its counterstory, the story of what it means to be a Palestinian in the occupied territories, subjected to hundreds of regulations of the bureaucratic microphysics of power — say, a Palestinian farmer is allowed to dig a hole in the earth no deeper than three feet to find a source of water, while a Jewish farmer is allowed to dig as deep as he wants.

A similar clash of narratives is at the very core of Christianity. One of the few remaining truly progressive U.S. publications, the *Weekly World News,* reported on a recent breathtaking discovery:[4] archaeologists discovered an additional ten commandments, as well as seven "warnings" from Jehovah to his people; they are suppressed by the Jewish and Christian establishment because they clearly give a boost to today's progressive struggle, demonstrating beyond doubt that God took a side in our political struggles. Commandment 11 is: "Thou shalt tolerate the faith of others as you would have them do unto you." (Originally, this commandment was directed at the Jews who objected to the Egyptian slaves joining them in their exodus to continue to practice their religion.) Commandment 14 ("Thou shalt not inhale burning leaves in a house of manna where it may affect the breathing of others") clearly supports the prohibition of smoking in public places; commandment 18 ("Thou shalt not erect a temple of gaming in the desert, where all will become wanton") warns of Las Vegas, although it originally referred to individuals who organized gambling in the desert close to the camp of wandering Jews; commandment 19 ("Thy body is sacred and thou shalt not permanently alter thy face or bosom. If thy nose offends thee, leave it alone")

4. "The Ten Commandments Were Just the Beginning . . . ," *Weekly World News,* November 6, 2006, pp. 24-26.

points toward the vanity of plastic surgery, while the target of commandment 16 ("Thou shalt not elect a fool to lead thee. If twice elected, thy
punishment shall be death by stoning") is clearly the reelection of Presi-
dent Bush. Even more telling are some of the warnings: the second warning ("Seek ye not war in My Holy Lands, for they shall multiply and afflict
all of civilization") presciently warns of the global dangers of the Middle
East conflict, and the third warning ("Avoid dependence upon the thick
black oils of the soil, for they come from the realm of Satan") is a plea for
new sources of clean energy. Are we ready to hear and obey God's word?

There is a basic question to be raised here, above the ironic satisfaction provided by such jokes: Is the search for supplementary commandments not another version of the search for the counterbook without
which the principal book remains incomplete? And insofar as this book-
to-be-supplemented is ultimately the Old Testament itself, is the
counterbook not simply the New Testament itself? This would be the
way to account for the strange coexistence of two sacred books in Christianity: the Old Testament, the book shared by all three "religions of the
book," and the New Testament, the counterbook that defines Christianity and (within its perspective, of course) completes the book, so that we
can effectively say that "the construction itself of the Bible is supported
by the junction between the two Testaments." This ambiguous
supplementation-completion is best encapsulated in the lines on the fulfillment of the law from Jesus' Sermon on the Mountain, in which he rad-
icalizes the commandments:

> You have heard that it was said to the people long ago, "Do not mur-
> der, and anyone who murders will be subject to judgment." But I tell
> you that anyone who is angry with his brother will be subject to judg-
> ment. . . . You have heard that it was said, "Do not commit adultery."
> But I tell you that anyone who looks at a woman lustfully has already
> committed adultery with her in his heart. . . . You have heard that it
> was said, "Eye for eye, and tooth for tooth." But I tell you, Do not resist
> an evil person. If someone strikes you on the right cheek, turn to him
> the other also. And if someone wants to sue you and take your tunic,
> let him have your cloak as well. If someone forces you to go one mile,
> go with him two miles. Give to the one who asks you, and do not turn

away from the one who wants to borrow from you. (Matt. 5:21-22, 27-28, 38-42 NIV)

The official Catholic way to interpret this series of supplements is the so-called double-standard view, which divides the teachings of the Sermon into general precepts and specific counsels: obedience to the general precepts is essential for salvation, but obedience to the counsels is necessary only for perfection, or, as Saint Thomas Aquinas put it (paraphrasing *Didache* 6.2): "For if you are able to bear the entire yoke of the Lord, you will be perfect; but if you are not able to do this, do what you are able." In short, law is for everyone, while its supplement is for the perfect only. Martin Luther rejected this Catholic approach and proposed a different two-level system, the so-called two-realms view, which divides the world into the religious and secular realms, claiming that the Sermon applies only to the spiritual: in the temporal world, obligations to family, employers, and country force believers to compromise; thus a judge should follow his secular obligations to sentence a criminal, but inwardly he should mourn for the fate of the criminal.

Clearly, both these versions resolve the tension by introducing a split between the two domains and constraining the more severe injunctions to the second domain. As expected, in Catholicism this split is externalized into two kinds of people, the ordinary ones and the perfect (saints, monks, etc.), while Protestantism internalizes the split between how I interact with others in the secular sphere and how I inwardly relate to others. Are these, however, the only ways to read this operation? A (perhaps surprising) reference to Richard Wagner might be of some help here: to his draft of the play *Jesus of Nazareth,* written between late 1848 and early 1849. What Wagner attributes here to Jesus is a series of alternate supplementations of the commandments:

> The commandment saith: Thou shalt not commit adultery! But I say unto you: Ye shall not marry without love. A marriage without love is broken as soon as entered into, and who so hath wooed without love, already hath broken the wedding. If ye follow my commandment, how can ye ever break it, since it bids you to do what your own heart and soul desire? — But where ye marry without love, ye bind yourselves at

variance with God's love, and in your wedding ye sin against God; and this sin avengeth itself by your striving next against the law of man, in that ye break the marriage-vow.[5]

The shift from Jesus' actual words is crucial here: Jesus "internalizes" the prohibition, rendering it much more severe (the law says no actual adultery, while I say that if you only covet the other's wife in your mind, it is the same as if you already committed adultery; etc.); Wagner also internalizes it, but in a different way — the inner dimension he evokes is not that of intention to do it, but that of love that should accompany the law (marriage). The true adultery is not to copulate outside of marriage, but to copulate in marriage without love: the simple adultery just violates the law from outside, while marriage without love destroys it from within, turning the letter of the law against its spirit. So, to paraphrase Brecht yet again: what is a simple adultery compared to (the adultery that is a loveless) marriage! It is not by chance that Wagner's underlying formula "marriage is adultery" recalls Proudhon's "property is theft" — in the stormy 1848 events, Wagner was not only a Feuerbachian celebrating sexual love, but also a Proudhonian revolutionary demanding the abolition of private property; so no wonder that, later on the same page, Wagner attributes to Jesus a Proudhonian supplement to "Thou shalt not steal!": "This also is a good law: Thou shalt not steal, nor covet another man's goods. Who goeth against it, sinneth: but I preserve you from that sin, inasmuch as I teach you: Love thy neighbour as thyself; which also meaneth: Lay not up for thyself treasures, whereby thou stealest from thy neighbour and makest him to starve: for when thou hast thy goods safeguarded by the law of man, thou provokest thy neighbour to sin against the law."[6] This is how the Christian "supplement" to the Book should be conceived: as a properly Hegelian "negation of negation," which resides in the decisive shift from the distortion of a notion to a distortion constitutive of this notion, i.e., to this notion as a distortion-in-itself. Recall again Proudhon's old dialectical motto "property is theft": the "negation of negation" is here the

5. Richard Wagner, *Jesus of Nazareth and Other Writings* (Lincoln and London: University of Nebraska Press, 1995), p. 303.

6. Wagner, *Jesus of Nazareth*, pp. 303-4.

shift from theft as a distortion ("negation," violation) of property to the dimension of theft inscribed into the very notion of property (nobody has the right to fully own means of production; their nature is inherently collective, so every claim "this is mine" is illegitimate). The same goes for crime and law, for the passage from crime as the distortion ("negation") of the law to crime as sustaining law itself, i.e., to the idea of the law itself as universalized crime. One should note that, in this notion of the "negation of negation," the encompassing unity of the two opposed terms is the "lowest," "transgressive," one: it is not crime that is a moment of law's self-mediation (or theft that is a moment of property's self-mediation); the opposition of crime and law is inherent to crime, law is a subspecies of crime, crime's self-relating negation (in the same way that property is theft's self-relating negation). And does ultimately the same not go for nature itself? Here, "negation of negation" is the shift from the idea that we are violating some natural balanced order to the idea that imposing on the Real such a notion of balanced order is in itself the greatest violation . . . which is why the premise, the first axiom even, of every radical ecology is "there is no Nature."

These lines cannot but evoke the famous passages from *The Communist Manifesto* that answer the bourgeois reproach that Communists want to abolish freedom, property, and family: it is the capitalist freedom itself that is effectively the freedom to buy and sell on the market and thus the very form of unfreedom for those who have nothing but their labor force to sell; it is the capitalist property itself that means the "abolition" of property for those who own no means of production; it is the bourgeois marriage itself that is universalized prostitution. In all these cases the external opposition is internalized, so that one opposite becomes the form of appearance of the other (bourgeois freedom is the form of appearance of the unfreedom of the majority, etc.). However, for Marx, at least in the case of freedom, this means that Communism will not abolish freedom but, by way of abolishing the capitalist servitude, bring about actual freedom, the freedom that will no longer be the form of appearance of its opposite. It is thus not freedom itself that is the form of appearance of its opposite, but only the false freedom, the freedom distorted by the relations of domination. Is it not, then, that, underlying the dialectic of the "negation of negation," a Habermasian "normative" approach imposes here immediately: How can we talk about crime if we do not have a preceding notion of legal order violated by the criminal transgression? In other words, is the notion of law as universalized/self-negated crime not auto-destructive? This, precisely, is what a properly dialectical approach rejects: what is before transgression is just a neutral state of things, neither good nor bad (neither property nor theft, neither law nor crime); the balance of this state of things is then violated, and the positive norm (law, property) arises as a secondary move, an attempt to counteract and contain the transgression. With regard to the dialectic of freedom, this means that it is the very "alienated, bourgeois" freedom that creates the conditions and opens up the space for "actual" freedom.

This Hegelian logic is at work in Wagner's universe up to *Parsifal*, whose final message is a profoundly Hegelian one: the wound can be healed only by the spear that smote it ("Die Wunde schliesst der Speer nur der Sie schlug"). Hegel says the same thing, although with the accent shifted in the opposite direction: the Spirit is itself the wound it tries to heal, i.e., the wound is self-inflicted.[7] That is to say, what is "Spirit" at its most elementary? The "wound" of nature: subject is the immense — absolute — power of negativity, of introducing a gap/cut into the given-immediate substantial unity, the power of differentiating, of "abstracting," of tearing apart and treating as self-standing what in reality is part of an organic unity. This is why the notion of the "self-alienation" of Spirit (of Spirit losing itself in its otherness, in its objectivization, in its result) is more paradoxical than it may appear: it should be read together with Hegel's assertion of the thoroughly nonsubstantial character of Spirit: there is no *res cogitans*, no thing that (as its property) also thinks, spirit is nothing but the process of overcoming natural immediacy, of the cultivation of this immediacy, of withdrawing-into-itself or "taking off" from it, of — why not? — alienating itself from it. The paradox is thus that there is no Self that precedes the Spirit's "self-alienation": the very process of alienation creates/generates the "Self" from which Spirit is alienated and to which it then returns. (Hegel here turns around the standard notion that a failed version of x presupposes this x as their norm (measure): x is created, its space is outlined, only through repetitive failures to reach

7. G. W. F. Hegel, *Aesthetics*, vol. 1 (Oxford: Oxford University Press, 1998), p. 98.

it.) Spirit self-alienation is the same as, fully coincides with, its alienation from its Other (nature), because it constitutes itself through its "return-to-itself" from its immersion into natural Otherness. In other words, Spirit's return-to-itself creates the very dimension to which it returns. (This holds for all "return to origins": when, from the nineteenth century onward, new nation-states were constituting themselves in central and eastern Europe, their discovery and return to "old ethnic roots" generated these roots.)

What this means is that the "negation of negation," the "return-to-oneself" from alienation, does not occur where it seems to: in the "negation of negation," Spirit's negativity is not relativized, subsumed under an encompassing positivity; it is, on the contrary, the "simple negation" that remains attached to the presupposed positivity it negated, the presupposed Otherness from which it alienates itself, and the "negation of negation" is nothing but the negation of the substantial character of this Otherness itself, the full acceptance of the abyss of Spirit's self-relating that retroactively posits all its presuppositions. In other words, once we are in negativity, we never quit it and regain the lost innocence of Origins; it is, on the contrary, only in "negation of negation" that the Origins are truly lost, that their very loss is lost, that they are deprived of the substantial status of that which was lost. The Spirit heals its wound not by directly healing it, but by getting rid of the very full and sane Body into which the wound was cut. It is a little bit like in the (rather tasteless version of the) "first the bad news then the good news" medical joke: "The bad news is that we've discovered you have severe Alzheimer's disease. The good news is the same: you have Alzheimer's, so you will already forget the bad news when you will be back home."

In Christian theology, Christ's supplement (the repeated "But I tell you . . .") is often designated as the "antithesis" to the thesis of the law — the irony here is that, in the proper Hegelian approach, this antithesis is synthesis itself at its purest. In other words, is what Christ does in his "fulfillment" of the law not the law's *Aufhebung* in the strict Hegelian sense of the term? In its supplement, the commandment is both negated and maintained by way of being elevated/transposed into another (higher) level. This is why one should reject the commonplace reproach that cannot but arise here: Is, from the Hegelian standpoint, the "second

story," this supplement that displaces the "first story," not merely a negation, a split into two, which needs to be negated in its own turn in order
to bring about the "synthesis" of the opposites? What happens in the
passage from "antithesis" to "synthesis" is not that another story is
added, bringing together the first two (or that we return to the first story,
which is now rendered more "rich," provided with its background): all
that happens is a purely formal shift by which we realize that the "antithesis" ALREADY IS "synthesis." Back to the example of class struggle: there
is no need to provide some encompassing global narrative that would
provide the frame for both opposing narratives: the second narrative
(the story told from the standpoint of the oppressed) ALREADY IS the
story from the standpoint of social totality — why? The two stories are
not symmetrical: only the second story renders the antagonism, the gap
that separates the two stories, and this antagonism is the "truth" of the
entire field.

Bibliography

Althusser, Louis. "Freud and Lacan." In Althusser, *Lenin and Philosophy, and Other Essays*. New York and London: Monthly Review Press, 1971.

Aquinas. *Summa Theologiæ*. 61 vols. London and New York: Blackfriars, 1964-81.

Arbaugh, George E., and George B. Arbaugh. *Kierkegaard's Authorship*. London: George Allen and Unwin, 1968.

Badiou, Alain. *Saint Paul: The Foundation of Universalism*. Translated by R. Brassier. Stanford: Stanford University Press, 2003.

Balthasar, Hans Urs von. *The Glory of the Lord*. Vol. 5, *The Realm of Metaphysics in the Modern Age*. Edinburgh: T. & T. Clark, 1991.

Band, Arnold, ed. *Nahman of Bratslav: The Tales*. New York: Paulist, 1978.

Barker, J. *Alain Badiou: A Critical Introduction*. London: Pluto, 2002.

Barzilai, Shuli. *Lacan and the Matter of Origins*. Stanford: Stanford University Press, 1999.

Baudrillard, Jean. *Seduction*. Translated by Brian Singer. New York: St. Martin's Press, 1990.

Beach, Edward. *The Potencies of God(s): Schelling's Philosophy of Mythology*. Albany: SUNY Press, 1994.

Beattie, Tina. *New Catholic Feminism*. London and New York: Routledge, 2006.

Beira, Mario. "Lacan, Psio-análisis y el Dios de Moisés." In *Lacan en Estados Unidos*, edited by Donna Bentolila-Lopez. Rosario, Argentina: Homo Sapiens, 1989.

Blanton, Ward. "Disturbing Politics: Neo-Paulinism and the Scrambling of Religious and Secular Identities." *Dialog* 46, no. 1 (2007): 3-13.

Blondel, Maurice. *Action: Essay on a Critique of Life and a Science of Practice*. Translated by Oliva Blanchette. Notre Dame, Ind.: University of Notre Dame Press, 1984.

Boothby, Richard. *Freud as Philosopher*. London and New York: Routledge, 2001.

Bottum, J. "Girard among the Girardians." *First Things* 61 (1996): 42-45. Available at http://www.leaderu.com/ftissues/ft9603/articles/revessay.html (accessed August 16, 2007).

Boucher, Geoff. "The Law as Thing: Žižek and the Graph of Desire." In *Traversing the Fantasy: Critical Responses to Slavoj Žižek,* edited by G. Boucher, J. Glynos, and M. Sharpe. Aldershot: Ashgate, 2005.

Boucher, Geoff, J. Glynos, and M. Sharpe, eds. *Traversing the Fantasy: Critical Responses to Slavoj Žižek.* Aldershot: Ashgate, 2005.

Bouillard, H. *Blondel and Christianity.* Translated by J. Somerville. Washington: Corpus Books, 1969.

Boyton, Robert. "Enjoy Your Žižek: An Excitable Slovenian Philosopher Examines the Obscene Practices of Everyday Life, Including His Own." *Linguafranca* 26 (March 2001). Available at http://www.lacan.com/Žižek-enjoy.htm (accessed August 22, 2007).

Breger, Claudia. "The Leader's Two Bodies: Slavoj Žižek's Postmodern Political Theology." *Diacritics* 31, no. 1 (2001): 73-90.

Butler, Judith, Ernesto Laclau, and Slavoj Žižek. *Contingency, Hegemony, Universality: Contemporary Dialogues on the Left.* London and New York: Verso, 2000.

Butler, Rex. *Slavoj Žižek: Live Theory.* London: Continuum, 2005.

Chamberlain, Lesley. *The Philosophy Steamer.* London: Atlantic Books, 2006.

Coward, H., and T. Foshay, eds. *Derrida and Negative Theology.* Albany: SUNY Press, 1995.

Cunningham, Conor. *Genealogy of Nihilism.* London: Routledge, 2002.

———. "Nothing Is, Something Must Be: Lacan and Creation from No One." In *Theology and the Political,* edited by Creston Davis, John Milbank, and Slavoj Žižek. Durham, N.C., and London: Duke University Press, 2005.

Dawkins, R. *The God Delusion.* London: Black Swan, 2007.

Depoortere, Frederiek. "The End of God's Transcendence? On Incarnation in the Work of Slavoj Žižek." *Modern Theology* 23, no. 4 (2007): 497-523.

Derrida, Jacques. *Acts of Religion.* Translated by S. Weber. Edited by Gil Anidjar. New York: Routledge, 2001.

———. *The Gift of Death.* Translated by David Wills. Chicago: University of Chicago Press, 1995.

———. "How to Avoid Speaking: Denials." In *Derrida and Negative Theology,* edited by H. Coward and T. Foshay. Albany: SUNY Press, 1992.

Freud, Sigmund. *Standard Edition of the Complete Psychological Works of Freud.* Edited and translated by James Strachey, in collaboration with Anna Freud, assisted by Alix Strachey and Alan Tyson. 24 vols. London: Hogarth Press, 1953-1974. See within this work the following: *Civilisation and Its Discontents* (1930 [1929]), 21:57-146; *Extracts from the Fleiss Papers* (1892-1899), 1:175-282; "The Infantile Genital Organisation: An Interpolation into the Theory of Sexuality" (1923), 19:141-48; *Introductory Lectures on Psychoanalysis* (continued)

(1916-1917), vol. 16; *Moses and Monotheism* (1939), 23:1-139; "My Views on the Part Played by Sexuality in the Aetiology of the Neurosis" (1905), 7:271-82; "The Question of Lay Analysis" (1926), 20:179-251; *Studies on Hysteria* (1893-1895), 2:1-252; *Totem and Taboo* (1913 [1912-1913]), 13:1-162; "The Uncanny" (1919), 17:217-52.

Gallagher, Cormac. "Overview of the Psychoanalytic Act." *The Letter: Lacanian Perspectives on Psychoanalysis,* 2000, pp. 104-14.

————. "A Reading of *The Psychoanalytic Act* (1967-1968)." *The Letter: Lacanian Perspectives on Psychoanalysis,* 2000, pp. 1-22.

Gay, Peter. *A Godless Jew: Freud, Atheism, and the Making of Psychoanalysis.* New Haven and London: Yale University Press, 1987.

Giard, Luce, "Michel de Certeau's Biography, Petite Bibliographie en anglais, par Luce Giard." http:/www.jesuits.com/histoire/certeau.htm (accessed August 17, 2007).

Girard, René. *Things Hidden since the Foundation of the World.* Translated by Stephen Bann and Michael Metteer. Stanford: Stanford University Press, 1987.

————. *Violence and the Sacred.* Translated by P. Gregory. London and New York: Continuum, 2005.

Glejzer, Richard. "Lacan with Scholasticism: Agencies of the Letter." *American Imago* 54, no. 2 (1997): 105-22.

Griffiths, Paul J. "Christ and Critical Theory." *First Things,* August/September 2004. Available at http://www.firstthings.com/article.php3?id_article=372 (accessed October 10, 2007).

Hallward, Peter, ed. *Think Again: Alain Badiou and the Future of Philosophy.* London: Continuum, 2004.

Hankey, W., and D. Hedley, eds. *Deconstructing Radical Orthodoxy: Postmodern Theology, Rhetoric, and Truth.* Aldershot: Ashgate, 2005.

Hart, Kevin. *The Trespass of the Sign: Deconstruction, Theology, and Philosophy.* Cambridge: Cambridge University Press, 1989.

Healy, Nicholas. *Thomas Aquinas: Theologian of the Christian Life.* Aldershot: Ashgate, 2003.

Hegel, G. W. F. *Aesthetics.* Vol. 1. Oxford: Oxford University Press, 1998.

Heidegger, Martin. *Being and Time.* Translated by J. Macquarrie and E. Robinson. Oxford: Blackwell, 1983.

————. "The Onto-theo-logical Constitution of Metaphysics." In *Identity and Difference,* translated by Joan Stambaugh. San Francisco: Harper and Row, 1974.

————. "The Thing." In *Poetry, Language, Thought,* translated by Albert Hofstadter. New York: Harper and Row, 1975.

Herman, Mark. *Brassed Off.* Channel Four Films, 1996.

Heschel, Susannah. "Reading Jesus as a Nazi." In *A Shadow of Glory: Reading the*

New Testament after the Holocaust, edited by Tod Linafelt. London: Routledge, 2002.

Irigaray, Luce. "Divine Women." In *French Feminists on Religion: A Reader,* edited by M. Joy et al. London and New York: Routledge, 2002.

Jameson, Fredric. "The Vanishing Mediator; or, Max Weber as Storyteller." In *The Ideologies of Theory: Essays, 1971-1986.* Vol. 2. London: Routledge, 1988.

Jantzen, Grace. *Becoming Divine: Towards a Feminist Philosophy of Religion.* Manchester: Manchester University Press, 1998.

Jennings, Theodore, Jr. *Reading Derrida/Thinking Paul.* Stanford: Stanford University Press, 2006.

Jones, James. *Religion and Psychology in Transition: Psychoanalysis, Feminism, and Theology.* New Haven and London: Yale University Press, 1996.

Kant, Immanuel. *Critique of Pure Reason.* Translated by J. M. D. Meiklejohn. London: Everyman, 1993.

—————. *Grounding for the Metaphysics of Morals.* Translated by J. W. Ellington. Indianapolis: Hackett, 1993.

Kay, Sarah. *Žižek: A Critical Introduction.* Cambridge: Polity, 2003.

Kerr, Fergus. "Simplicity Itself: Milbank's Thesis." *New Blackfriars* 861 (1992): 306-10.

Kierkegaard, Søren. *The Concept of Anxiety.* Translated by R. Thomte. Princeton: Princeton University Press, 1980.

—————. *Concluding Unscientific Postscript.* Vol. 1. Translated by H. Hong and E. Hong. Princeton: Princeton University Press, 1992.

—————. "On the Difference between a Genius and an Apostle." In *The Present Age,* translated by Alexander Dru. London: Fontana, 1962.

—————. *Philosophical Fragments.* Edited and translated by H. Hong and E. Hong. Princeton: Princeton University Press, 1985.

—————. *Repetition/Fear and Trembling.* Translated by H. Hong and E. Hong. Princeton: Princeton University Press, 1983.

Labbie, E. *Lacan's Medievalism.* Minneapolis: University of Minnesota Press, 2006.

Lacan, Jacques. *Autres Écrits.* Paris: Seuil, 2001.

—————. *Écrits.* Paris: Seuil, 1966.

—————. *Écrits.* Translated by Bruce Fink. New York and London: Norton, 2006.

—————. "Introduction to the Names-of-the-Father Seminar." In *Television: A Challenge to the Psychoanalytic Establishment,* edited by Joan Copjec and translated by Jeffrey Mehlman. New York and London: Norton, 1990.

—————. *Le Séminaire Livre VIII: Le Transfert, 1960-1961.* Edited by Jacques-Alain Miller. Paris: Seuil, 1991.

—————. *The Seminar of Jacques Lacan: The Knowledge of the Analyst* (1971-1972). Translated by Cormac Gallagher. Unpublished.

—————. *The Seminar of Jacques Lacan: The Logic of Phantasy* (1966-1967). Translated by Cormac Gallagher. Unpublished.

————. *The Seminar of Jacques Lacan, I: Freud's Papers on Technique, 1953-1954.* Edited by Jacques-Alain Miller. Translated by John Forrester. London and New York: Norton, 1991.

————. *The Seminar of Jacques Lacan, II: The Ego in Freud's Theory and in the Technique of Psychoanalysis, 1954-1955.* Edited by Jacques-Alain Miller. Translated by Sylvana Tomaselli. London and New York: Norton, 1991.

————. *The Seminar of Jacques Lacan, III: Psychosis, 1955-1956.* Edited by Jacques-Alain Miller. Translated by Russell Grigg. London: Routledge, 2000.

————. *The Seminar of Jacques Lacan, V: The Formations of the Unconscious, 1957-1958.* Translated by Cormac Gallagher. Unpublished.

————. *The Seminar of Jacques Lacan, VII: The Ethics of Psychoanalysis, 1959-1960.* Edited by Jacques-Alain Miller. Translated by Dennis Porter. London: Routledge, 1999.

————. *The Seminar of Jacques Lacan, XI: The Four Fundamental Concepts of Psycho-analysis, 1963-1964.* Edited by Jacques-Alain Miller. Translated by Alan Sheridan. London: Vintage, 1998.

————. *The Seminar of Jacques Lacan, XV: The Psychoanalytic Act* (1967-1968). Translated by C. Gallagher. Unpublished.

————. *The Seminar of Jacques Lacan, XVI: From the Other to the Other* (1968-1969). Translated by C. Gallagher. Unpublished.

————. *The Seminar of Jacques Lacan, XX: On Feminine Sexuality; The Limits of Love and Knowledge, 1972-1973.* Edited by Jacques Alain-Miller. Translated by Bruce Fink. London and New York: Norton, 1998.

————. *Television: A Challenge to the Psychoanalytic Establishment.* Edited by Joan Copjec. Translated by Jeffrey Mehlman. New York and London: Norton, 1990.

————. *Le Triomphe de Religion/Discours auc Catholiques.* Paris: Seuil, 2005.

Laclau, Ernesto. *New Reflections on the Revolution of Our Time.* London: Verso, 1990.

Laplanche, Jean, and Jean-Bertrand Pontalis. *The Language of Psychoanalysis.* Translated by D. Nicholson-Smith. London: Karnac Books, 1988.

Larval-subjects. Available at http://larval-subjects.blogspot.com/2006_01_larval-subjects_archive.html (accessed June 12, 2007).

Lefort, Claude. *The Political Forms of Modern Society.* Cambridge: Polity, 1986.

Lippitt, John. *Kierkegaard and Fear and Trembling.* London: Routledge, 2003.

Lubac, Henri de. *The Mystery of the Supernatural.* New York: Crossroad, 1998.

————. "Spiritual Understanding." Translated by Luke O'Neill. In *The Theological Interpretation of Scripture: Classic and Contemporary Readings,* edited by Stephen Fowl. Oxford: Blackwell, 1997.

Mannoni, Octave. *Clefs pour l'Imaginaire ou l'Autre Scène.* Mayenne: Seuil, 1985.

Marenbon, John. "Aquinas, Radical Orthodoxy and the Importance of Truth." In *Deconstructing Radical Orthodoxy: Postmodern Theology, Rhetoric, and Truth,* edited by W. Hankey and D. Hedley. Aldershot: Ashgate, 2005.

McClelland, J. S. *A History of Western Political Thought.* London and New York: Routledge, 1996.

Milbank, J. *Being Reconciled: Ontology and Pardon.* London: Routledge, 2003.

―――. "Materialism and Transcendence." In *Theology and the Political: The New Debate,* edited by C. Davis, J. Milbank, and S. Žižek. Durham, N.C., and London: Duke University Press, 2005.

―――. *The Suspended Middle: Henri de Lubac and the Debate concerning the Supernatural.* Grand Rapids and Cambridge: Eerdmans, 2005.

―――. *Theology and Social Theory.* 2nd ed. Oxford: Blackwell, 2006.

Milem, Bruce. "Four Theories of Negative Theology." *Heythrop Journal* 48 (2007): 187-204.

Miller, Jacques-Alain. "The Inexistent Seminar." Translated by Philip Dravers. *Psychoanalytic Notebooks* 15 (2005): 9-42.

―――. "Profane Illuminations." *Lacanian Ink* 28 (2007): 12-13.

Nietzsche, F. *The Gay Science.* Translated by J. Nauckhoff. Cambridge: Cambridge University Press, 2001.

―――. *Twilight of the Idols/The Anti-Christ.* Translated by R. Hollingdale. London: Penguin Books, 2003.

Parekh, B. "The Rushdie Affair and the British Press: Some Salutary Lessons." In *Free Speech.* Commission for Racial Equality, 1990.

Parker, Ian. *Slavoj Žižek: A Critical Introduction.* London: Pluto, 2004.

Pfaller, Robert. "Where Is Your Hamster? The Concept of Ideology in Žižek's Cultural Theory." In *Traversing the Fantasy: Critical Responses to Slavoj Žižek,* edited by G. Boucher, J. Glynos, and M. Sharpe. Aldershot: Ashgate, 2005.

Pickmann, Claude-Noële. "Examining a Clinic of the Not-All." *The Letter: Lacanian Perspectives on Psychoanalysis,* Spring 2004, pp. 19-30.

Pickstock, Catherine. *After Writing: On the Liturgical Consummation of Philosophy.* Oxford: Blackwell, 1998.

Plato. *Meno.* Translated by W. K. C. Guthrie. Middlesex: Penguin Books, 1981.

Pseudo-Hadewijch. *Poesie Miste.* Translated and edited by Alessia Vallarsa. Genoa and Milan: Marietti, 2006.

Rice, Emanuel. *Freud and Moses: The Long Journey Home.* Albany: SUNY Press, 1990.

Richardson, William. "'Like Straw': Religion and Psychoanalysis." *The Letter: Lacanian Perspectives on Psychoanalysis* 11 (1997): 1-15.

―――. "Psychoanalysis and the Being-question." In *Psychiatry and the Humanities: Interpreting Lacan,* vol. 6, edited by J. Smith and W. Kerrigan. London: Yale University Press, 1983.

Roazen, Paul. "Lacan's First Disciple." *Journal of Religious Health* 4 (1996): 321-36.

Robert, Martha. *From Oedipus to Moses: Freud's Jewish Identity.* Translated by Ralph Manheim. New York: Anchor Books, 1976.

Rose, Gillian. *Hegel contra Sociology.* London: Athlone, 1981.

Roudinesco, Elisabeth. *Jacques Lacan.* Translated by Barbara Bray. London: Polity, 1999.

———. "Psychoanalysis and Homosexuality: Reflections on the Perverse Desire, Insult and the Paternal Function." *Journal of European Psychoanalysis,* no. 15 (Fall/Winter 2002); www.psychomedia.it/jep/number15/roudinesco.htm (accessed August 19, 2007).

Schmitt, C. *Political Sovereignty: Four Chapters on the Concept of Sovereignty.* Translated by G. Schwab. London: MIT Press, 1985.

Scorsese, Martin. *The Last Temptation of Christ.* DVD, 1989. Universal Pictures, Universal Studios, 1998.

Sharpe, Matthew. *Slavoj Žižek: A Little Piece of the Real.* Aldershot: Ashgate, 2004.

Shepherdson, Charles. Foreword to *Lacan's Seminar on "Anxiety": An Introduction,* by Roberto Harari. Translated by Jane Lamb-Ruiz. New York: Other Press, 2001.

Smith, James. *Jacques Derrida: Live Theory.* New York and London: Continuum, 2005.

———. *Speech and Theology: Language and the Logic of Incarnation.* London and New York: Routledge, 2002.

Stavrakakis, Yannis. "The Lure of Antigone: *Aproias* of an Ethics of the Political." In *Traversing the Fantasy: Critical Responses to Slavoj Žižek,* edited by G. Boucher, J. Glynos, and M. Sharpe. Aldershot: Ashgate, 2005.

Stephens, Scott. "Žižek, My Neighbour — regarding Jodi Dean's *Žižek's Politics.*" *International Journal of Žižek Studies* 1 (2007). Available at http://zizekstudies .org/index.php/ijzs/issue/view/2 (accessed August 29, 2007).

Turkle, Sherry. "Tough Love: An Introduction to Francoise Dolto's *When Parents Separate.*" Available at http://web.mit.edu/sturkle/www/dolto.html (accessed August 16, 2007).

Wagner, Richard. *Jesus of Nazareth and Other Writings.* Lincoln and London: University of Nebraska Press, 1995.

Wilden, Anthony. *The Language of the Self.* Baltimore: Johns Hopkins University Press, 1968.

Williams, J., ed. *The Girard Reader.* New York: Herder Crossroads, 2001.

Williams, Rowan. "Between Politics and Metaphysics: Reflection in the Wake of Gillian Rose." *Modern Theology* 11, no. 1 (1995): 3-22.

———. *On Christian Theology.* Oxford: Basil Blackwell, 2000.

Wright, Elizabeth, and Edmond Wright. *The Žižek Reader.* Oxford: Blackwell, 1999.

Žižek, Slavoj. *The Abyss of Freedom/Ages of the World by F. W. J. Schelling.* Ann Arbor: University of Michigan Press, 1997.

———. *The Art of the Ridiculous Sublime: On David Lynch's "Lost Highway."* Seattle: Walter Chapin Simpson Centre for the Humanities, 2000.

———. "Concesso non Dato." In *Traversing the Fantasy: Critical Responses to Slavoj*

Žižek, edited by G. Boucher, J. Glynos, and M. Sharpe. Aldershot: Ashgate, 2005.

———. *Did Somebody Say Totalitarianism? Five Interventions in the (Mis) Use of a Notion.* London and New York: Verso, 2001.

———. *Enjoy Your Symptom: Jacques Lacan in Hollywood and Out.* 2nd ed. London and New York: Routledge, 2001.

———. *For They Know Not What They Do: Enjoyment as a Political Factor.* London and New York: Verso, 2002.

———. *The Fragile Absolute; or, Why Is the Christian Legacy Worth Fighting For?* London and New York: Verso, 2000.

———. *The Fright of Real Tears: Krzysztof Kieslowski between Theory and Post-Theory.* London: British Film Institute, 2001.

———. *How to Read Lacan.* London: Granta Books, 2006.

———. "Human Rights and Its Discontents: Olin Auditorium Bard College, November 15, 1999." http://www.lacan.com/zizek-human.htm (accessed March 15, 2008).

———. *The Indivisible Remainder: An Essay on Schelling and Related Matters.* London and New York: Verso, 1996.

———. "The Inherent Transgression." *Cultural Values* 1 (1998): 1-18.

———. *Interrogating the Real.* Edited by Rex Butler and Scott Stephens. London and New York: Continuum, 2005.

———. "An Interview with Slavoj Žižek, 'On Divine Self-Limitation and Revolutionary Love,'" by Joshua Delpech-Ramey. *Journal of Philosophy and Scripture.* Available at http://www.philosophyandscripture.org/Issue1-2/Slavoj_Žižek/slavoj_Žižek.html (accessed August 16, 2007).

———. *Iraq: The Borrowed Kettle.* London and New York: Verso, 2004.

———. "'It Doesn't Have to Be a Jew': Žižek Interviewed by Josefina Ayerza." *Lusitania* 4 (1994). Available at http://www.lacan.com/perfume/Žižekinter.htm (accessed August 19, 2007).

———. "Lacan in Slovenia: An Interview with Slavoj Žižek and Renata Salecl." *Radical Philosophy* 58 (1991): 25-31.

———. *Looking Awry: An Introduction to Jacques Lacan through Popular Culture.* Cambridge and London: MIT Press, 1991.

———. *The Metastasis of Enjoyment: Six Essays on Woman and Causality.* London: Verso, 1994.

———. *On Belief.* London: Routledge, 2001.

———. *Organs without Bodies: On Deleuze and Consequences.* London and New York: Routledge, 2004.

———. *The Parallax View.* London: MIT Press, 2006.

———. *The Plague of Fantasies.* London and New York: Verso, 1997.

————. "A Plea for a Return to *Différance* (with a Minor *Pro Domo Sua*)." *Critical Inquiry* 32 (2006): 226-49.

————. *The Puppet and the Dwarf: The Perverse Core of Christianity*. London: MIT Press, 2003.

————. "Robespierre, or, the Divine Violence of Terror." In *Žižek Presents Robespierre: Virtue and Terror*, edited by J. Ducange and translated by J. Howe. London and New York: Verso, 2007.

————. *The Sublime Object of Ideology*. London and New York: Verso, 2002.

————. *Tarrying with the Negative: Kant, Hegel, and the Critique of Ideology*. Durham, N.C.: Duke University Press, 1993.

————. *The Ticklish Subject: The Absent Centre of Political Ontology*. London and New York: Verso, 2000.

————. *The Universal Exception*. Edited by Rex Butler and Scott Stephens. London and New York: Continuum, 2006.

————. *Virtue and Terror: Slavoj Žižek Presents Robespierre*. Edited by J. Ducange. Translated by J. Howe. London and New York: Verso, 2007.

————. *Welcome to the Desert of the Real*. London and New York: Verso, 2002.

————. "What If the Other Is Stupid?" In *Think Again: Alain Badiou and the Future of Philosophy*, edited by P. Hallward. London and New York: Continuum, 2004.

————. "Why Should a Dialectician Learn to Count to Four?" *Radical Philosophy* 58 (1991): 3-9.

————. "Woman Is One of the Names-of-the-Father." *Lacanian Ink* 10 (1995). Available at http://www.lacan.com/zizwoman.htm (accessed July 16, 2007).

————, ed. *Cogito and the Unconscious*. Durham, N.C., and London: Duke University Press, 1998.

————, ed. *Everything You Always Wanted to Know about Lacan (but Were Afraid to Ask Hitchcock)*. London and New York: Verso, 2000.

————, ed. *Lacan, the Silent Partners*. London and New York: Verso, 2006.

————, ed. *Revolution at the Gates: Selected Writings of Lenin from 1917*. London and New York: Verso, 2002.

Žižek, Slavoj, and Glyn Daly. *Conversations with Žižek*. Cambridge: Polity, 2004.

Žižek, Slavoj, and Mladen Dolar. *Opera's Second Death*. London: Routledge, 2002.

Zwart, H. "Medicine, Symbolisation and the 'Real' Body." *Journal of Medicine, Healthcare, and Philosophy* 1 (May 1998).

Index